Please Plant This Book
Coast To Coast

a memoir by

Susan Kay Anderson

Finishing Line Press
Georgetown, Kentucky

Please Plant This Book
Coast To Coast

Finalist, Panther Creek Award for Nonfiction, Hidden River Arts 2018

Copyright © 2021 by Susan Kay Anderson
ISBN 978-1-64662-487-4 First Edition
All rights reserved under International and Pan-American Copyright Conventions.
No part of this book may be reproduced in any manner whatsoever without written permission from the publisher, except in the case of brief quotations embodied in critical articles and reviews.

ACKNOWLEDGMENTS

Grateful Acknowledgement is given to the following editors and staff of these publications where parts of this manuscript first appeared in slightly different form:

Arthur Magazine: "'Freedom?': Richard Brautigan's first wife, Virginia Aste, speaks in a new interview"

Beat Scene: "Oaxaca"

Linocut #3 of Please Plant This Book Coast To Coast (orange and black) was part of an invitational exhibit in Denver, Colorado in the spring of 2016, "State of Unions" at the Ice Cube Gallery, Dry Ice Factory (curated by Jean B. Smith, et al).

Linoleum cut prints and photos of Virginia Brautigan Aste are by Susan Kay Anderson. Other photos of various memorabilia and of Virginia Brautigan Aste are courtesy of Virginia Brautigan Aste.

Permission granted to re-print "Please Plant This Book" by the estate of Richard Brautigan.

Publisher: Leah Huete de Maines
Editor: Christen Kincaid
Cover Art: Virginia Brautigan Aste
Author Photo: Susan Kay Anderson
Cover Design: Elizabeth Maines McCleavy

Order online: www.finishinglinepress.com
also available on amazon.com

Author inquiries and mail orders:
Finishing Line Press
P. O. Box 1626
Georgetown, Kentucky 40324
U. S. A.

Table of Contents

Sea Lion Caves 1

Some of the Unspoken 4

The Past Real 7

Trout Fishing In America 11

In The Afternoon 12

B Vitamins 13

To Say The Least 14

Into The Creek 15

A Great Fan 17

Rexburg, Reseda 20

The Daily Bruin 23

A New York Minute 31

Before Going To Another Coast 38

Like A Waterfall 40

Oaxaca 43

Please Plant This Book 52

Camping 55

Hawaii 59

Afterward 66

For Here: On Interviewing Virginia Brautigan Aste 80

Dear Noeli 89

The Crooked House 97

Sex In History by Reay Tannehill 116

Through The Looking Glass 123

Notes & Thanks 136

Index of Images 138

*Virginia Brautigan Aste
at the Ginny Aste Skate Park, Ceremony of Naming & Dedication
Pahoa, Hawaii, 2018*

Virginia Brautigan Aste at the Ginny Aste Skatepark in Pahoa, Hawaii, 2015

Virginia Brautigan Aste, Black Rock Café, Pahoa, Hawaii, 2015

Virginia Bratuigan Aste, Black Rock Café, Pahoa, Hawaii, May, 2009

Virginia Brautigan Aste, Black Rock Café, Pahoa, Hawaii, May, 2009

Virginia Brautigan Aste, Black Rock Café, Pahoa, Hawaii, 2009

Coasting is so easy. To coast through life. I went into a store [in New York] and borrowed a dime for the subway; it was too cold to walk. My coat wasn't that warm. I returned the dime later and the store owner laughed and laughed—he didn't really expect me back.

I kept that stupid coat. It wrapped around me
.

***

We painted our floor orange and all the furniture black in our apartment [in San Francisco]. We had two Siamese cats. We lived there, off of unemployment or our tax refund. Somehow, there was always money. Things didn't cost as much as now. It was so different then. I had unemployment up to two weeks before Ianthe was born.

***

Mort Hytner said he was going to marry Mary (of Peter, Paul, and Mary). I think they were married for about six weeks. I lost track of him. He was an intense writer. I gave them a present of a tea pot with decoration like the colors of a Siamese cat as a present.

***

There were U.C.L.A. hanger-ons trying to get their novels published.

***

The first school Ianthe attended was the Raspberry School in San Francisco. It was in a store front in San Francisco. The second school Ianthe (and later Ellen) went to was the Frobel School. It was in the redwoods in a church camp. They used Cuisenaire Rods there. The trees were beautiful. You could just walk a little ways into the forest and be with the trees.

Sea Lion Caves

It has been almost a year since Virginia and I went to visit Sea Lion Caves on the Oregon Coast in the fall of 2019. We are now in the middle of a pandemic and climate emergency. The crucial voicing of protest against authoritarian rule and inequity is sharply amplified by conditions made more dangerous by the deadly Covid-19 virus as the world rights itself in order to be healed and sane. Nearly coinciding with the rise of deaths due to this pandemic has been an escalation of violence by police toward citizens, especially those stopped by police who are black; those who are vulnerable to an armed intervention at protests in support of the Black Lives Matter movement have been gassed, grabbed, kidnapped, beaten and killed. What is chaotic escalation is also fierce organization. What is the environmental crisis is also a building force for positive change in nearly every aspect of our lives. This book couldn't be timelier. Virginia's story never more poignant and instructive.

When we visited Sea Lion Caves there were no sea lions inside the huge sea cave, the enormous ocean cavern where hundreds gather in the winter months to escape the cold. Instead, they were basking outside on some nearby cliffs, blending into the rocky precipices. We learned that the sea lions residing there are actually ones who migrated up from Fisherman's Warf in San Francisco, now settled at Sea Lion Caves. It seemed we chose the perfect place to visit, the best place to say hello to.

What we found was different than what we thought, but no less important. We found the sun and wind and ocean breezes. We found the view. The sea lions' need to escape to a peaceful and safe haven was understandable. Being gawked at inside a cave is probably better than being gawked at in San Francisco. From stable city piers to a wildly tossing sea inside the cave and watery environs.

Virginia is no stranger to upheaval and change. The archipelago of the Hawaiian Islands is an extremely dynamic landscape because of its active volcanoes. This is where Virginia lives. She had to move a dozen times due to lava and hurricanes.

A little about this book: It has been more than a decade since I began interviewing Virginia and is more accurately nearing a decade and-a-half. She is 86 at the time of this writing and just recently stopped working as a substitute teacher. Dear Reader, you will see that she always was in it for the long haul.

In *The Order Of Time*, by Carlo Rovelli (Penguin/Random House, 2018), he writes: "…We are struggling to adapt our language and our intuition to a new discovery: the fact that the 'past' and 'future' do not have a universal meaning. Instead, they have a meaning that changes between here and there. That's all there is to it." (Rovelli, 113)

Please Plant This Book Coast To Coast not only fills gaps in the history of the Beats, but exemplifies the typical attitudes, lifestyle choices, and thinking of the era. It paints a compassionate view yet serves as a gentle counterpoint to Ianthe Brautigan's *You Can't Catch Death, A Daughter's Memoir* (St. Martin's Press, 2000). It also uncovers Virginia's influence and bears witness to one of the Beat era's most unique writers, warts and all: Richard Brautigan. If you've read the recently published *Jubilee Hitchhiker: The Life And Times Of Richard Brautigan*, by William Gatz (Counterpoint Press, 2012), then this book will open your eyes up to the sweetness of the era, and the sweetness of the woman he married before he was famous, instead.

Samples of Virginia's Feminist Studies and Sociology research papers, written in the 1980's when Virginia returned to college, are included. Readers familiar with Brautigan will enjoy discovering someone influential to his vision and success (Virginia lugged home a typewriter from work every day to type up his manuscripts) and will also marvel at her unique expressions and anecdotes as she almost channels his quirky outlook and phrasing.

This is the personal memoir of Virginia Brautigan Aste. She remembers growing up in California, attending U.C.L.A., living in N.Y., meeting and marrying Richard Brautigan, and eventually moving to Hawaii, where she now resides. What is here are descriptions of events, people, and places vital to the complete history of Beat writers. This is the story of the woman who nurtured, supported, and launched one of America's most innovative and beloved writers: the man who explored and struck gold in the frontier claim of Carp Press.

Thank you for reading this book, for picking it up and wandering through its pages. It is my hope that you will not only gain a new appreciation for Richard Brautigan's writing, but also consider the influence Virginia has had on American Literature.

Susan Kay Anderson
Sutherlin, Oregon
August 13, 2020

Some of the Unspoken

Richard Brautigan called me, "the woman who travels with me" in his writing, after I objected to "my old lady" the popular term at the time. He was the one who wanted to get married. I was in love but ambivalent about marriage. I never really thought I'd get married. My parents stayed together for thirty years. They were so miserable. I often wished my mother would just leave. The idea of being married was not a commitment, but a sentence. I never felt the need to be married. I thought it would be enough when people were committed. That's why I was so shocked when Richard turned violent towards me.

I recently read Joyce Carol Oates', "A Widow's Story," (December, 13, 2010, *The New Yorker*). I was very touched by her writing, and the reason it was so clear to me, was that there is so much unspoken in a marriage. One thinks it will be said, but it isn't. When that person is gone or the marriage has died, it is too late. Coast to Coast is what I have to say that I did not. It is some of the unspoken that I would like to say now.

We held the idea of Bohemia or the New Age or the Love Era as a chance encounter that might or might not last. We inspired each other. He lived in a rarified world of painters and poets. They accepted him and didn't think he was strange but other people thought him odd. We travelled together and saw things that were familiar yet not.

Growing up, I did not travel until I was 15. I got my chance the first time I crossed the United States with my friend Joan. Her mother had hooked up with a WWII Vet who had a hairtrigger temper. Joan's younger brother, Joan, Joan's mom, and Joe drove all the way to the Grand Canyon that summer. It was astounding. For the better part of a day, at the Grand Canyon, Joni's little brother stopped being a brat. When we got to Iowa and out to Joe's parents' farm, it was sold and they were moving into town, his mom cooked an angel food cake on the wood stove. So we got just a little bit of what farm life could be like. I remember thinking—it was August and hot—how uncomplicated it was, but how difficult and time consuming. I also remember thinking, God, what if you had to do this in the winter!

In the small Iowa town, my most vivid memory of that was that some of the boys were holding hands. The only other place I saw that was in Oaxaca, later when I was an adult. The boys who were left behind were too young to go to the Korean War. They had jobs like detassling the corn or skinning bullheads [fish].

The town had a lost feeling to it. No vitality. Ten or fifteen minutes out of town, the prairie made a huge impression on me. I had read *Little House on the Prairie*. The farm was more like Little House on the Muddy Farm.

I remember the endless card games in the back of the car. Across Nebraska and Kansas the corn was eight feet high. In Kansas there were rolling hills but when we got to flat Nebraska, Lincoln, Nebraska, rose out of the green. It looked like the Manhattan skyline. It looked like this big city. Lots of grain elevators. Like Oz. Grey buildings.

I remember the isolation of the farms. Later, I would see it, in Andrew Wyeth's painting of "Christina's World." I remember thinking of my grandmother because she described Kansas and Nebraska as nothing but wheat fields. Because the corn obliterated the fences, it appeared to be a sea of just one crop. It was one immense feature.

My grandmother lived in that kind of isolated land. Kids had to walk six or eight miles to school. My uncle had a damaged ankle from when his horse ran him into a barbed wire fence. It affected his gait. This was normal. If you lived in Lincoln, or Kansas City, you could get to a hospital, at least. Helicopters hadn't been invented yet.

This trip was really an exploration—the beginning of my interest in travel. What my grandmother experienced as a woman growing up became real to me. I saw that both coasts were built on the product of the Midwest. Even after the dustbowl. It had come back. The sustainability was always on my mind. I always questioned, was it sustainable? Did they just gobble up all those small farms for a purpose? There is a movement to go back to small farms now.

These sensibilities were what I brought to my relationship with Richard.

When we went on our trip to Idaho, Richard always got in the picture. I would be getting ready to take a photo of an old car or a tree and he would step into the frame and pose in a Napoleonic way. It was not as a little kid would do, in a teasing way, but as if I had intended on taking the picture of him (even though I had not). He was always checking himself if he passed a mirror, and looked at his hair, clothes, not in a vain way, but I think to see if he was still there. It was almost as if he was thinking he would disappear at any moment.

One minute he'd be posing, one minute singing to Ianthe, one minute checking to see if he was still there.

The trip would have been called My Tour On A Greyhound Bus [instead of *Trout Fishing In America*] if we had not done it together, because, I bought the station wagon and I was the one who drove.

My life was always about the moment and the next and whether it was on a cross-country trip with a child, or helping someone with a novel or poem. I was always thinking, what is the point? You don't see that till afterwards.

Back then, we asked ourselves, what are the principles that guide you? For us, it was always poverty, truthfulness, and simplicity. This is the artist's viewpoint, the distillation of existence.

The Past, Real

Man's Fate

Please Plant This Book Coast To Coast #1

A Boat

O beautiful
was the werewolf
in his evil forest.
We took him
to the carnival
and he started
crying
when he saw
the Ferris wheel.
Electric
green and red tears
flowed down
his furry cheeks.
He looked
like a boat
out on the dark
water.

> —Richard Brautigan
> *The Pill Versus the Springhill Mine Disaster* (1968)

Werewolf And Boat

Trout Fishing In America

I met Richard Brautigan at a Laundromat in North Beach.

I had wanted to meet him. He was very alluring and I thought he might've been from Germany. He didn't say much. I had Ron Loewinsohn introduce us.

Richard was working in a lab that manufactured different flavored barium powder. People drank the powders for X-rays—there were different flavors like peach, strawberry, lemon. He came home smelling like those different flavors. They hired Richard for one dollar an hour.

I was working downtown as a secretary. I carried the typewriter home with me. It was very heavy. I typed up his poems. He began sending them out to places like *The Nation*. He started with fifty poems.

I was working for two dollars an hour. I was good at Dictaphone. From our tax return and claiming Ianthe as a dependent, we bought a 1951 Plymouth station wagon and took a trip across Idaho, five hundred or six hundred miles across the Snake River. This became *Trout Fishing In America*. Jack Spicer helped edit it. I helped edit, too, and typed it because I could read Richard's handwriting. I was used to it, and from reading lots of [scrawly] doctor and lawyer handwriting.

In the Afternoon

He would write in the afternoon because he watched Ianthe in the morning.

That became a routine because I was working. He needed time and space, time and silence, but not totally, he did not lock himself away.

Richard would read us stuff, and Jack Spicer or I would tell him to take out a lot. There wasn't much left. That was Spicer's thing.

He read incessantly at the Mechanics' Institute Library. It was a library founded by a union in San Francisco. He'd read fiction on the 2nd floor. He'd read the *Ladies Home Journal.*

He told me his earliest reading was the *National Geographic.* He read old issues when he was in elementary school. He read Faulkner, Jack London, he read poetry.

I translated Neruda's work for him into English, also, Mayakovsky's. I took Russian so I could translate Russian poetry. A lot of people were killed under Stalin. People still talked a lot about the Spanish Civil War in those days and we knew at least two men who had gone to Spain to fight.

B Vitamins

Richard was a genius in his writing because of his humor.

He was like Mark Twain or Saroyan because of his use of irony, he would be right on target.

He also had a sense of the tragic. He had sentimentality for his dead relatives but he was never syrupy sweet in that way.

He was very caring, cared very well for Ianthe. He paid the rent six months in advance before she was born. Had a stockpile of food in the cupboards. Probably because he cared for his sister, Barbara, while they were growing up. He had grown up very poor. I almost got him sobered up. I gave him a lot of B vitamins. After our baby came, he began drinking heavily again, lots of socializing.

I read on the internet that he had had homosexual liaisons at this time. It was when Ianthe was about four. I don't know if I believe that.

He had new fame, it was tremendously exciting. He began drinking heavily and became abusive. One night, he wanted to have sex and became violent. When I refused, I shut him out of the bedroom. There were these thick wooden doors—the next day I left with Ianthe.

What happened was totally against what we were all about. We were so pacifistic. This was the dark side of what was going on. On the other hand, he did love guns and loved going shooting.

To Say the Least

He had a constant dialog going and had constant jokes.

He was interested in everything about art. Dada was one of the themes. Jack Spicer said that one should pick out the worst thing of a piece of writing and keep that and then write from that. He told Richard that and sometimes he did that.

He was experimental like William Burroughs and the same that he traveled around and eventually had a huge following. Burroughs would tear a page of his writing down the middle and then match up the halves to different pages, creating interesting sentences, to say the least. Richard never did that, but he matched and mismatched images. His poems are like a time capsule.

I think Richard was very sad when I left him, taking Ianthe with me. People didn't talk about addiction, about drinking then. Oh, I should've…maybe stuck with him, gotten…it was a few years later when the lawyer had me sign for a divorce. I didn't make any claim to his work.

In his early books, I know exactly what and where he is talking about—even though the writing is ambiguous on purpose. I can picture this or that place. I can picture every place in: *In Watermelon Sugar, Trout Fishing In America, and The Abortion, A Romance*, exactly.

Once we lived in Big Sur, in a cave that was carved out of a hill with a little roof jutting out of it to keep the rain off. He was very interested in the history of WWI and WWII. He loved reading about the Civil War. He was particularly interested in the campaigns of the southern generals. He talked about the Holocaust. He was fascinated with the personalities surrounding Hitler and in the atrocities dictated by the S.S.

Into the Creek

He was very interested in graveyards, gravestones.

Interested in imagining what people's lives were like—the food they ate, the clothes, one hundred and two hundred years ago. He was interested in the working people.

On our trip to Idaho, we read gravestones in old cemeteries.

He was always connecting different times and people and places together. He did this constantly, made connections. He had a maniacal laugh, Ianthe has the same, a real wild laugh.

In '57-'58, we did crazy things. Climbed up on the Palace of Fine Arts and looked over the city—all the heads of statues toppled over.

Once, with Kenn Davis, who was selling paintings at the time, we went to a reading—the hood of our car flew off at one o'clock in the morning as we approached the Bay Bridge. Richard jumped out of the car, opened the trunk and threw it in. He could move really really fast when he had to.

We were cooped up inside five days once in Big Sur. Up a little creek. Water came down and we could not get up to the highway. He jumped into the creek and got me. He never could swim, but he was capable of athletic feats nobody thought he could do.

In Big Sur, Richard was very interested in Price Dunn, who was the Confederate General of Big Sur [from book of the same name]. Price read the Greek Classics, as a child in Alabama. He took us down to Big Sur. We were two or three weeks there. We talked, fixed meals, had two cases of wine. I remember there was an invasion of frogs there. The wine had soured, so we poured wine around the porch to try to kill the frogs to stop their noise. They were kind of like the coquis in Hawaii.

As one of my friends said about Richard, 'he was like shining too bright a light on too small a thing.' His writing was not voluminous. By the time it got pared-down, and pared-down, there weren't a lot of words. There wasn't a lot to work with.

He was good at listening to criticism. He worked with and listened to Ron Loewinsohn, an academic and a poet. He wasn't like Robert Duncan who was a traditional poet, or Kenneth Rexroth, who was a target for Beat poets because he was so academic, but was well-published.

Richard was contemptuous of literature taught in college. He got to become the flavor-ofthe-month for a lot of them. He liked the Black Mountain College poets [Creeley, Dorn, Olson]. Richard knew Lawrence Ferlinghetti, who appreciated his work from the beginning. Ferlinghetti was very supportive of Richard, he liked him and helped him. Also, Mr. Diamond, the lawyer who I worked for. He allowed me to type up Richard's poems, got me stamps to send them out. Very helpful.

Artist Tom Field was a really neat guy. He lived with us for awhile and was an inspiration to Richard. He taught Ianthe drawing when she was four.

A Great Fan

In "All Watched Over By Machines of Loving Grace," Richard anticipated the impact of computer technology.

He was happy to get an electric typewriter. It was a lot of work making corrections on copies of his work, and typing it over and over. It took a lot of time.

He would've been a great fan of the word processor because he couldn't spell. I think he ran out of things to write about, unlike Styron and Mailer—who he didn't like.

Alcohol shut down his spontaneity and depressed him and accelerated/exaggerated the parts of his personality that was pessimistic about people. I'm pretty sure he did not believe in god or an afterlife. He believed in art and the arts as the highest people could live for.

Please Plant This Book Coast To Coast #4

I was supposed to launder the old socks and send them in with the guarantee. Right off the bat, new socks would be on their way, traveling across America with my name on the package. Then all I would have to do, would be to open the package, take those new socks out and put them on. They would look good on my feet.

I wish I hadn't lost that guarantee. That was a shame. I've had to face the fact that new socks are not going to be a family heirloom. Losing the guarantee took care of that. All future generations are on their own.

—Richard Brautigan, *Trout Fishing In America*

Rexburg. Reseda.

I was born at home in Rexburg, Idaho, July 11, 1934.

It was in 1934 that my parents took a trip and went to the Chicago World's Fair. When I was six weeks old, they left me. They were gone a few weeks, taking the train to Chicago. My mother was twenty-eight when they married, my father was forty-five. She was the baby, really, and he was showing her the world. I was left in the care of an aunt.

They were living out their dream of the 1920's. They had riding clothes, deluxe camping equipment, and a new car. Mother travelled from Nampa, Idaho [then] every summer to San Jose to attend a teacher's college. It took her many summers to get her degree. She taught school in Nampa until she married.

Dad had been a banker and farmer. When I was a year old, we went to California to live with my Uncle and Aunt because my father's bank had failed and the price of wool and potatoes was so low he could not continue farming. We came in a 1936 Chevrolet that was paid off and he sold the ranch (in Idaho) and paid off the bank depositors. We lived in Reseda in the San Fernando Valley.

I was the oldest; I have just one brother who is four years younger. He and I grew up with a girl cousin. She was kind of mean and loved playing outside. I had asthma, I wasn't outdoorsy, I loved to read. She would practically tear the book out of my hands because she wanted me to play outside.

There is a picture of my tenth birthday party in Reseda; my brother is not yet in the picture. He was born in Van Nuys, six miles from there.

When we came to Southern California my dad tried real estate. He had been in the Marine Corps., and tried to re-enlist as a pilot, but he was too old. He worked as a parking lot attendant and janitor in Van Nuys. He was 47 and he was broke. There were no jobs. He was ahead of his time, having been a pilot, anticipating the real estate boom in Southern California, but unable to wait until it came. All my father was left with was his car.

Dad was born in 1896 and had lived a full life before the Great Depression hit. He became very depressed. Alcohol was always a problem.

He probably started drinking in the Marine Corps. The nearest college was in Stamford, Nebraska. My father went to two years of college there.

He was a brilliant man, never earned a degree, but he flew planes, and finally had a job with Radioplane in California. He wasn't an engineer, but he made things there. He never wanted my mother to work. He would not allow it. Victorian ideals. After my brother was born, we then went to live with my uncle and aunt (father's brother). My uncle had come to Reseda with the dregs of his bank and my grandmother's savings. They bought a quarter acre in Reseda and planted trees and a garden which my aunt and grandmother tended. They continued farm traditions, in part because there was very little money. I learned to kill and de-feather chickens, pick apricots, can all kinds of vegetables and make grape jam.

My father got out of college and enlisted in the Navy, two years' experience, and then he was offered a commission in the Marines if he'd go to Pensacola, Florida to train for the War in 1917. He flew precursors of the bombs of WWII, the pilot and co-pilot picking them up and dropping them over France and Germany.

Richard wrote a short story about this. He interviewed my father.

In California, they had the annual Kansas picnic and then the Nebraska picnic. People would get together in the park in Los Angeles. Oklahoma picnics later, I suppose, but the picnics were very territorial.

My great-grandfather brought grandmother to Kansas. As far as I can tell, his wife stayed in Germany. They homesteaded and got a chance to go to Nebraska to get more acreage on the prairie. He built them a sod house, it had an Isinglass window and a root cellar to be safe from tornadoes. My grandmother recalled when they hid from tornadoes. My father and two uncles and grandfather built a large house, a two story, when they were prosperous. They raised wheat, cattle. She had three boys and then two girls. The youngest girl died at age two. She named my father Grover Cleveland (Alder). She was a radical, my grandmother, and saved a newspaper which declared the abolition of slavery. Grandmother came at age 4 from Germany. She could read and write in fine German script. Grandfather established a farm in Kansas. They traveled in a covered wagon to a homestead in Nebraska. She translated for people from German to English. Uncle kept a big book, a photo album. It had been a sample book from a paint company. He had pictures of the two story house. They lived in Illinois before homesteading in Kansas and then went on to Nebraska—always acquiring more land.

My great-grandfather was a tyrant. Grandmother married a gentle man who died of the Spanish Flu in 1922. He was almost a non-person in the Jacobs family.

I identified with Grandmother my whole life.

She lived with my aunt and uncle. We lived with them and then got a house right across the street in Reseda.

Reseda had a hitching post in the center of town, across from the bank. It had a crossroads. There was the post office, the bank, the drug store, and a bar. Canoga Park—my high school—was surrounded by bean fields. Another little town was Northridge, which was the train station. We had a street car that came as far as Reseda. They tore it out while I was in high school. They've restored it now. The first thing I remember about Reseda was in second grade, the Carrera marble façade of Win's Drugstore, where I would read comics. There were many orchards of apricot and walnut trees.

After World War II, and the dust bowl movement to California, hundreds of houses were built, and aircraft workers who didn't want to go back to their home states bought them. At the end of World War II, there was overbuilding—Palmdale, for example, the whole town collapsed. To people who came from the mid-west, California was pleasant, no snow.

My parents then lived in the same house for 30 years. At one point, my cousins moved in with my uncle and aunt. A son and daughter-in-law and their daughter moved in. Grace, the daughter-in-law, was sick with pneumonia. She lived because her husband and my dad found a supply of penicillin. My aunt Grace worked in the drug store, she was the mother of the cousin from hell, the one who didn't let me read. The shining light was Grace. She was like her name, sweet, correct, and always there. She was a Mormon and my cousin was raised a Mormon. For a while the Mormon Bishop called repeatedly to invite me to the youth group.

My father was an atheist, my grandmother was a Methodist, and tried unsuccessfully to raise her sons and daughter as Methodists. My father explained to me what atheism and agnosticism meant and most of the church service seemed absurd to me.

The Daily Bruin

I didn't really leave home until about the second year of college.

I tried to commute to U.C.L.A. from the San Fernando Valley. Tuition was very cheap. It was about fifteen dollars a unit. Of course, that was a lot money then. Books were always expensive. That was always a big chunk. But, I had no role models, there were no counselors. The master's degree students that were grading the papers were never available—it was just in a way, a nightmare—it was like this faceless place with 27, 000 students. A "Streetcar University," they called it.

I graduated from Canoga Park High School in 1951. I was 16 and I started college right then, that fall. I started driving up over Sepulveda Pass back and forth. I went immediately, at age sixteen, to U.C.L.A. and enrolled.

I had no idea what I was doing. I had been told by the counselor that I wouldn't be given a scholarship because, "the girls won't need their scholarships because they're going to be getting married." So the three scholarships that were available were given to boys, even though I was the third, I think, in my class.

So I got on a campus with 250 to 300 students in my history class, the sociology class. Driving back and forth over Sepulveda Pass about nineteen miles each way each day. It was a pretty good drive. It just took a lot of time.

It was windy and rainy. And I was also working different places. I remember getting one job on campus in the entomology lab which lasted about a month. I accidently let a whole bunch of fruit flies out that were part of an experiment. And I almost died of boredom filling up these little test tubes with alcohol and putting these rubber stoppers in, and you push this little needle down the side and let the air out and you push the stopper down. Cases and cases of those.

Later I worked at a drive-in that served hamburgers. They flew the meat from Denver— and chocolate shakes; that was their big thing. I learned to carry trays on my hands, with my hands flat [to the sides, above the shoulders] and that ended when I dropped one of these heavy malt glasses on my toe; that was the end of that. Then, I got a job in a boat firm assembling blocks that hold sail lines. That was reasonably pleasant and paid well. That's what you did when you were in college, you know, you worked at different jobs. If I could've found anything on campus that would've been better—I just found that one job and sort of blew it. So, I was in over my head from the beginning with the history and sociology classes. I didn't understand how to study or how much time it would take or even what was expected of me. I don't remember going to the library at all, except maybe one or two times the first year.

It was just overwhelming. Some of the classes were huge. They were divided into sections with a teaching assistant for each of them and they were unapproachable graduate students. Just not friendly.

So I gravitated to *The Daily Bruin*. That was the second year I was there. I had two other friends that were going. One of them was pregnant and was trying to keep the child, the fetus inside her body and it didn't work. She eventually miscarried, but then she quit and went and married this guy and had three kids and lived happily ever after. And then the other one quit, too, end of the first year. She just couldn't, didn't want to do college. Both of them had enrolled in the teaching program, the education program. And, I looked at the textbooks, and I looked at the assignments given, and I knew that wasn't it. I don't know where the nursing program was then. I don't know how you got into it, I probably would've been o.k. with that, if I could've had an angel, you know, somebody shoving me into it. Yeah, maybe that might have worked. Then, when I got on the student newspaper, it was a daily paper, so every day was exciting.

Sometimes the people there were emotionally radical, and politically radical, too. So I became really fascinated. I did some writing. The paper was actually produced at a print shop in Santa Monica, off campus, with a linotype machine. So I learned all about that, how type was set in lead slugs. It just became a big part of my life. I started taking political science courses and they were tremendously interesting but I didn't have any idea how to study for them or how to write papers and exams.

I remember going to two different sororities. One was Tri Delta and they weren't interested in me at all. I forget what the other one was, and finally, I landed in a co-op. It was two duplexes with a little two room house in back. Again, heavily Jewish, but it was on Sorority Row.

There were no other dorms. There was no transportation, except by car. I ended up living off-campus in Santa Monica, in a little house in Venice with my friend Lenore Yanoff.

There I met a whole group of political radicals through Lester Rosenthal, a friend who reappeared several times in my life. Stuart Perkoff comes to mind, he's a poet who lived in Venice. There were others. A transvestite who could speak French and that was of value to me because I wanted to learn to speak French so I could read poetry. It was a constant struggle to try to figure out what kind of papers I was supposed to be writing and a struggle just to get to class—because the paper would be put to bed anytime between eleven and one a.m. I got paid for doing the newspaper so it was kind of an anchor, but, double sided, because it took up so much time, and then, I got into a romance, and sexual liaisons with several different people on the newspaper. One never knows. I have to think how to say this, but—it's my belief that I have some real disorders coming from my alcoholic family. My way of acting that out was sexual promiscuity and my way of looking for intimacy, companionship, love, acceptance, was sex. And of course it didn't help that we were approaching the 60's and that's what everybody thought was going to be o.k. And maybe it was for some people.

But, even now it has hurt me, kept me from being in contact with some of the people that are still part of that newspaper staff because I am so embarrassed about my conduct. It's true. I don't think there was really anything I could help. It was just a stage I had to go through. They had established relationships and I just sort of came on the scene. At the time I felt it was great.

My academic life went up, down, up, down. I met Mort Hytner, a writer who wanted to go to New York. I had a car and we went. We drove in three days to New York and that ended four years at U.C.L.A. not because I got a degree, but because I just left. I also thought that I would also be able to get some kind of job in publishing. College. There weren't a lot of women, really, who attended college. It was more young men. Later, it was returning Korean Vets. That was sort of a new thing for women to do, go to college, I mean, for America. It seemed like they were all men, on the G.I. Bill, from World War II and the Korean War. What happened was, I gravitated towards the student newspaper, which was an incredible collection of people.

I wrote for the high school paper and I wrote essays. The problem with the newspaper was that it didn't really get started until one in the afternoon, and then it was write it and get it together and then take it to the print shop and you really didn't get through until eleven at night and then I would have to drive back home. *The Daily Bruin* became like a part-time job. If you were the night or desk editor, you got paid. But I was fascinated by the people. I started smoking so I could play a game called Raunch, which was putting a napkin on top of a paper cup. You could sit in the cafeteria. Then, you lit a cigarette; put a penny on the napkin. And then you'd burn a little strip, and someone else would burn a little strip. It sounds insane. And then the person who made the penny drop would buy the next round of coffee. Most of the people on the paper were Jewish. There was a fraternity and sorority row, but no dorms—it was a very divided campus in a lot of ways. It was my introduction to Judaism. Also, there was a heavy anti-communist trip on campus. A *Bruin* reporter, the son of one of the editors of *The Daily News* in downtown Los Angeles, George Garrigues, was under surveillance and denied editorship of *The Daily Bruin*, just because his father was suspected of being a communist. Hearst owned the other paper, *The Examiner*, and was trying to drive *The Daily News* out of business and *The Daily News* was just barely liberal.

At that time, anything that was barely liberal was suspected of being communist.

He wrote a book. I've never read it, but he wrote a book about those times. And there was another person, Fredy Perlman, who wrote about those times.

George became editor, later. Yeah, but just because his father was under suspicion, he became under suspicion and it became a terrible battle to get the editor approved by the student council, and the student council were mostly preppy fraternity boys.

That was a unique time. There was such a fear of communism and of course anti-Semitism. And so we would just have these struggles and it didn't help that we published stories that were about the fact that the student council had allocated $300 each for rings for themselves. But that newspaper ran twelve to sixteen pages every day and it received extremely high awards across the nation from journalism departments. My dilemma was that there was no journalism department; there were just two classes, taught by a writer, Robert Kirsch, I took those two classes, and that was it, I couldn't major in journalism.

I went with Lenore, my roommate, and Jerry Farber, both English majors from U.C.L.A., to Big Sur where we visited with Henry Miller. He fed us onion soup in the middle of a huge rainstorm. We stayed there and he sent us along with some packages to mail, maybe to get rid of us. He trusted us with those packages, and they were probably manuscripts.

The Daily Bruin office was a center for writers on campus. The English Department was very traditional.

I didn't consider myself a writer. Later, Richard told me my writing wasn't any good, I shouldn't quit my day job. Of course, the day job was what was supporting him.

I saw myself as a journalist but I wasn't too good at it. I wrote some play reviews and one summer I covered tennis. I had really very little training. The people who took the editorship of that paper—a couple of them were crazy, brilliant, but crazy. One of them had Tourette's syndrome, I think. They were strange kids and some not-so kids, they were older. And in the office next door, there was a National Student Association plant, a guy, that we were convinced was a spy of some sort.

We thought he was keeping an eye on the newspaper because the student council would know things before we knew them. I had a very difficult time. I didn't understand most of the lectures. I had no background in European history at all. I had no idea the Holocaust had happened until my roommate [Lenore] wouldn't speak to me for three days because I said something to the effect that, well, they probably did something that the government didn't like.

Some utterly stupid thing. Lenore, who was Jewish, later took me to meet her parents, introduced me to Kosher foods and we learned more about Jewish history.

It was really extremely intense. At one point there was a protest because Eugene Debs, a socialist, wanted to speak in Royce Hall which held about 1,000 people. He was barred from speaking there and had to speak at the Y.W.C.A., which only held 150 seats. The F.B.I. was watching the campus, and the student council seriously, and it was a struggle to keep the spectrum of political opinion open, so at least you could talk about what was going on. And so you could participate enough to see whether you as a student even wanted to join an organization like Students For A Democratic Society. In my little rinky-dink high school, my teacher, Mrs. Bettington, was fired for being a communist. Even this little high school was a victim of the McCarthy scene.

I wore a purple corduroy duster for awhile. It was later in San Francisco that black became the uniform; tights and jerseys.

I was just 16. My friends on the newspaper, Al Frank and Tony Myrup-Frank took me to hear jazz. They later got married and had two really beautiful children—and he made a fortune in penny stocks. Tony lived in Eagle Rock, near Pasadena, and they took me to this tiny little jazz club where Chet Baker and Thelonius Monk, all the jazz greats started and I wasn't 18, I wasn't 21. I would slip in there trying to look older and order a Shirley Temple and we listened to that jazz. God, that was wonderful. That was a really wonderful time.

I don't know who owned that place. How it became a jazz club—maybe the artists just came because they had a venue. There were never more than fifty people in the place. Little tiny tables. No lines. It was like no one knew the musicians yet. It was an exciting time. It was just the beginning of an era and in trying to do all those things, I kept flunking out of school.

So I flunked out, and went to Santa Monica City College. Now, the irony of that was, I was a political science major, and the same professor that I managed to get a B from but didn't really understand too well in his European History course—and I don't even remember what era we were talking about—taught a class on World War II, and the Holocaust. Same guy, he'd been in Dachau, and that class had perhaps forty people in it, with eight or ten older people. I got an A plus because of the difference in class size, and the passion to learn about it. He was doing the lectures, not these snotty-nosed, master's degree pop stars that would have these office hours and then wouldn't be there. At any rate, I was having a hard time. I got back in U.C.L.A., I flunked out again, and then I left for New York and then that's a whole other story.

A long life. It really is a long life.

Please Plant This Book Coast To Coast #2

I talked to the surgeon for a little while longer and said good-bye. We were leaving in the afternoon for Lake Josephus located at the edge of the Idaho Wilderness, and he was leaving for America, often only a place in the mind.

—Richard Brautigan, *Trout Fishing In America*

A New York Minute

I did try a couple of things when I got to New York.

The first day I was there I got a job in a mosaic shop, so I was able to start work. In the village. The real problem was I couldn't find a place to live. The people who had the mosaic shop—one was Ned, he was a Harvard graduate, and had a cat that he had done all kinds of psychological tests on. He was just a great cat, a big yellow and white tabby cat named Sam. And there was Laura, who was a photographer, who looked a little bit like Jackie Kennedy, and they ran this mosaic shop and her idea was to make it arty and beautiful with inlaid mosaic coffee tables. His idea was to cut up the mosaics and put them on a stainless steel plate and sell them to the military for their crafts program.

So as fast as she would sell a table, he would use the money to buy steel saucers. But, one of Laura's touches was that there was a pot of Lapsang Souchong tea, and people would drop in on Friday night and Saturday afternoon for their mosaics to create their coffee table projects. And about once a month, a box of these small burlap bags would arrive, each with a beautiful color of tesserae, or mosaics. They were original mosaic tiles like the ones that they use in churches in Italy. And Ned, meanwhile, was cutting up these inch square mosaic tiles, glass tiles, that they had commercially manufactured for bathrooms and floors.

The different mosaics were kept separate, I would get to put them in order and label the colors and people could order them by the quarter pound. Different colors according to the designs. Meanwhile, Ned was working on his mosaic by the numbers on the steel plates, using the other kind that you soaked off the paper wrappings. I had this basement apartment, for eleven dollars a month. It was rent controlled. Very dark. It had a fifteen gallon hot water heater you had to light, in fact, you lit a burner, if you didn't turn it off, and it would steam up and explode.

I had this great cat, again, a cat, that used to come and go through an open window. I kept the window open all the time because of the gas from the hot water heater. I didn't know if it was going to blow me away or what. And because the cat needed to come in and out. He would come about once a week and eat and just lie around under the warmth of the hot water heater and then he would leave again. Finally, I got sick, and after that they took me into their apartment [Ned and Laura]. So then I was then privy to all their arguments and a lot of good dinners, Laura was a very good cook. Every Saturday when we closed the shop, which was usually one in the morning by the time we finished up our orders, we would pile in Ned's jeep and go get the *Sunday Times*, which weighed about three pounds. And then we'd bring it back and read until dawn and go to sleep for awhile and then wake up and have brunch or whatever, and plan the next week. They were really very kind to me.

But Lenore, an old friend, a really close friend from college showed up in New York, and we took off in the summer of '57, because I had been there awhile by then. We took a bus through Connecticut, and hitchhiked from there to Canada. We got a ride from the border to Montreal with the Prime Minister. A limousine stopped for us and picked us up and wanted to know what we were doing.

And, we went on to Montreal. We had walked along a bunch of beautiful roads. I remember I was carrying a copy of Malraux's *Man's Fate*, filling it with wildflowers, thinking I would keep them as a reminder of the trip, but all that happened was that all the pages became stuck together (it weighed about two pounds) and you couldn't open it because it was all stuck together with flowers. Nice idea. Beautiful landscape. It was really, really beautiful.

We stopped in Cape Cod on the way back and met this fisherman who invited us onto his boat. He was a Korean War vet with a lobster boat. He was pretty shook up, P.T.S.D., we would call it now, and he had chosen that as a way to get well. We helped winch up the lobster, weighed them, sized them and ate them when we stopped on an island in the bay.

At the border, six miles from it, we stayed at a B & B and Lenore started to speak French. We didn't know that some towns were English only. We thought we'd be murdered in our beds that night. It was a Green Giant town. The reason for the town was the Green Giant peas and beans. I guess they had taken over the town, it had been a French speaking town, and then became an English speaking town and there was a lot of tension and anger.

We got a ride to the bus depot and took the bus back. The reason we did that was because we were told that if we hitchhiked in Connecticut, we'd get arrested. That was really a trip, I mean, two girls hitchhiking alone, it was really pretty unique at that time.

When we returned, I got a job at Columbia University. That was where I found a place to live that was just a vestibule in the front of an apartment house. They had torn out the front to make it a new side stairway entrance. My friend Libby lived below in a rather warm basement apartment. I had this vestibule upstairs, and I had yards and yards of burlap that I had gotten as part of my severance from the mosaic shop. I tried to cushion—make it warm—because it was colder than hell in that little vestibule. It was about twelve feet wide and about sixteen feet. It was like an entry hall. But they were no longer using the front steps or the front entrance, so it had these French doors at the end. And it was just freezing. It was like an ice-box. So when I would get too cold, I'd go downstairs to Libby's apartment and warm up. Most of the time, it was o.k. I embarked on copying music. I thought that would be a good career. Never mind that I couldn't read music. David Williams paid me to copy his music and I did that for awhile. That was another wonderful idea.

My job at Columbia University was to get three bids on every pencil, every eraser, every bottle of ink, every box of carbon paper that Columbia University was going to use. There were these slips of green paper where we had to write the price for each item on the grid, then the next price, and the next. You'd mark down with the red pencil, and then the blue pencil, and regular pencils to write everything in. Then, you'd pick the one that was the least expensive, the lowest one from 25 items. Very tedious. But I got to take six units at Columbia. Three units in Greek Drama, and this theater critic taught a survey of comedy in English and American Drama, and that was kind of fun. His lectures were really funny.

So I did that for awhile, and then by that time I had met a friend who was much, much older than I was. Now I can see he reminded me of my father. We used to bicycle around New York and we took a couple of trips to Staten Island, got on the ferry, went around Staten Island. I remember one day I had my first orgasm on a bike. I didn't know what it was. I thought, wow, this is a good feeling.

Well, I'd had a lot of sex, but never had an orgasm, so that was kind of a revelation. But my friend, Sam Brody, who was then in his 70's—kids broke into his apartment which was the third floor apartment—right near where I was living in that funny little hallway. They stole his camera equipment, putting him out of business. He was a medical photographer. They took all his cameras. Such a mean thing to do. He lived on 103rd on the top floor. His name was Brody because his parents come from the Russian city of Brody. He spoke French. He was extremely animated and had a big head, fairly long, curly hair, compelling eyes, and a wild sense of humor. He carried my bike and Lenore's and had tea ready when we staggered up the stairs. I sure he didn't have any money saved. I'm not sure what he did for an income.

It finally—that second winter—I just thought, I don't want to be in New York anymore. The cold got to me.

I remember I went into Macy's one day. I didn't have a coat. I went into Macy's and I stole a wool tweed skirt and a really warm sweater, and I stole the wrong coat. I had that coat and I was stuck with it forever.

It was too ugly.

But I had that coat until I went to California and I even wore it the winter I was pregnant with Ianthe. It worked really well for that, walking around the coast wrapped in a brown coat with a yellow fleece lining.

I remember coming out of there, with the sweater and my skirt stuck in my leather bag and the coat on. I just ripped the tag off and walked out the door with it, feeling perfectly justified because I wasn't making enough money to buy winter clothing. Gloves. Never had decent food.

The second winter, I just thought, you know, this is stupid; this is not working very well. And Lenore had by that time gone back to San Francisco and had a place there. So that's where I went. I left Sam behind.

Lenore and I met at the Bagel Shop on Grant Street. That was the beginning of my experience in North Beach and that's where I met Richard.

Sam wrote me these letters, pleading with me to come back to New York, and so on.

He finally moved out to San Francisco, didn't have anything to do with me, met this other young woman, and had a baby with her. It was like, oh, Sam, what was your agenda? You know? [Laughter] It was a year later. So I left and was in San Francisco six weeks later, where I met Richard. He was pretty captivated by him [Sam], too. Sam's first wife was someone—he was with Alice Neel, the painter. I was so shocked that he had married and had a baby, later, when I saw him in San Francisco. After I was with Richard, he said he had met Sam Brody and told me, "He knew you." I saw them twice after this.

They came to a reading of Richard's. At Fugazi Hall. An Italian hall. It was a free or virtually free hall. Sam was still a full-on communist. That was the era in which the U.S. people thought folk dance, music, etc. were bringing people together. Nuclear weapons weren't a reality.

I do remember the contrast, in North Beach, how clean it was, compared to New York City. There was a tradition of chucking things into the street in San Francisco, so we'd go look for stuff in New York, too.

Please Plant This Book Coast To Coast #3

Less time than it takes to say it, less tears than it takes to die; I've taken account of everything, there you have it. I've made a census of the stones, they are as numerous as my fingers and some others; I've distributed some pamphlets to the plants, but not all were willing to accept them. I've kept company with music for a second only and now I no longer know what to think of suicide, for if I ever want to part from myself, the exit is on this side and, I add mischievously, the entrance, the re-entrance is on the other. You see what you still have to do. Hours, grief, I don't keep a reasonable account of them; I'm alone, I look out of the window; there is no passerby, or rather no one passes (underline passes). You don't know this man? It's Mr. Same. May I introduce Madam? And their children. Then I turn back on my steps, my steps turn back too, but I don't know exactly what they turn back on. I consult a schedule; the names of the towns have been replaced by the names of people who have been quite close to me. Shall I go to A, return to B, change at X? Yes, of course I'll change at X. Provided I don't miss the connection with boredom! There we are: boredom, beautiful parallels, ah! how beautiful the parallels are under God's perpendicular.

—Richard Brautigan

Before Going To Another Coast

Fredy Perlman enrolled at U.C.L.A. and had just come from Bolivia.

He turned up in New York. His parents came from Yugoslavia. When he turned up, I thought Fredy was going to kill Sam. Fredy and his wife went to Yugoslavia, later.

What was great about New York was when my friends went to Fire Island and I would watch their cat. They would be gone and hours before they got back their cat would sit at the door and wait like it knew they were coming.

"The Dada will remember what the I.B.M. forgets."

—Richard Brautigan

Like a Waterfall

The 60's were a lot like the 50's, a continuation of them.

Except for '68 and '69. Then, everything changed. For example, I took Lamaze classes prior Ianthe's birth. They didn't know what I was talking about when I arrived at the hospital.

They gave me some pillows and helped me lie on my side. That was that.

The change came with the music. There were concerts every day, really REALLY good concerts every two weeks or so. Groups from New York came. The concerts were in Golden Gate Park. In one house where we lived, there was something wrong with the plumbing so the water ran and ran. It was like a waterfall. We just got water or turned it stronger and then back again.

Richard admired the Diggers. Our whole thing was a proletarian idea that you take care of everybody. I remember baking bread in coffee cans. The Diggers did it. I did, too.

We had everything available to us at the Free Store. We never had any money. I don't remember paying for anything for a while. This was the last half of the 60's.

At that time there was the Cow Palace, a big stadium—George Wallace was to speak. All I remember—the atmosphere of hostility and women there, it was a feeling of a mob and impeding violence and we just had to leave. We went to that; Ianthe had gotten a new raincoat from her dad. This (Cow Palace) was a place where women burned their bras, where riots happened. Ianthe's raincoat pocket caught on a car as we were leaving and she started to cry. It was no real riot that time, but it felt like it could've been. What we were witnessing was a lot of yelling and Wallace was yelling back. He was ranting. It was an awful ending to an awful day.

We moved out of North Beach and out of Haight-Ashbury. There was a lot of alcohol and pot use. There was the Ice Cream Store where bikers and bus drivers took pills—early speed, the chicken egg producing drug, Methedrine—cheaper than heroin. It was the time of the Alphonse Mucha art style on concert posters—big bicycle wheels on bikes, elongated figures riding, and the skulls and roses of the Grateful

Dead.

For a year, there were free concerts every other week. It was wild—of course there were precursors to this pre-60's.

I purchased a Rudi Gernreich bra—it was see-through—and took off my shirt during a party. We saw how many people could crowd into a phone booth at a time. The phone booth was in a San Francisco loft south of Market Street.

Things were mystical then. I was with Tony and Richard was on the periphery when Ianthe was seven-eight years old and Ellen was two. There was this artist named John, a transplant from Salt Lake. They called him Coffee Table because he painted a series on old doors and sold them as coffee tables. He ran out of those and started painting on rocks. He used a jeweler's glass to paint. He came out one night and said if he had diamonds he could sell his art. I found a rhinestone necklace in the gutter and gave it to him. He put little 'diamonds' onto his paintings.

San Francisco

This poem was found written on a paper bag by Richard Brautigan in a laundromat in San Francisco. The author is unknown.

By accident, you put
Your money in my
Machine (#4)
By accident, I put
My money in another
Machine (#6)
On purpose, I put
Your clothes in the
Empty machine full
Of water and no
Clothes

It was lonely.

—Richard Brautigan

Oaxaca

We went to Mexico although I do not remember why.

We had two friends who were there, a married couple who were down there with their daughter who was named Claudia, who was about three or four years old. His name was John and I can't remember his wife's name. They were in Oaxaca and I think that's all we knew. It was very popular then to go to Mexico then because when we took that trip it was twelve pesos to the dollar. Later, it was eight. But the money exchange rate was good. I'm trying to remember how we got out, to Mexico, I think we took a car but to where? It must've been to Los Angeles and then we started hitch hiking.

Then, we hitch hiked to the border. We got a ride down there with a truck driver who took us all the way to Nogales. Then we got across the border and there was nothing scary about it, but it didn't seem like we were really going to get anywhere attractive, that would feel good, so, we took the third class bus and were so frightened of drinking the water and stuff, we drank so much soda pop that by the time we finally got to Mexico City, we were just both really sick. And we asked the taxi driver for a hotel and I can still remember going into that room with the strong smell of perfume and then yellow and magenta satin spread and pillow shams, so it must've been a whorehouse at night. So we very quickly became aware of the fact that tourists were pretty much at the mercy of whoever or whatever network the taxi drivers had.

We wandered around Mexico City, although it was very hard to understand what bus brought you where and so forth and I remember standing thunderstruck at a cathedral, watching women on their knees dragging across the courtyard, fingering their rosaries to the entrance to the cathedral. I had never seen that. Kneeling and just dragging along. All the way across the stony courtyard and on the posts of the wall surrounding the courtyard were skulls. Now, maybe I imagined that. I've always wanted to go back and see, are there really skulls on the posts holding the wall?

They were carved right into the posts. Inside I expected to see a cathedral that was as richly appointed as those in Europe, but it wasn't. It might be now, but it wasn't. Wooden doors, and then when we had come in on the bus, it was a tent and shack city for miles before we got into Mexico City.

At that time, it was probably six, seven million people.

That was in 1959, because when we got back, we decided to have Ianthe. She was born in
1960.

And then, after we left Mexico City, on the bus, it was a six, seven, eight hour trip to Oaxaca. I had read and studied about the revolution in Oaxaca, which was relatively recent. There were land struggles in Oaxaca. Not very much of Mexico is arable land, but Oaxaca, that whole valley has always been able to cultivate bushels and bushels of corn and all kinds of things.

We found a house down there. We were befriended by a dentist and he introduced us to Don Renento who had been the major land holder down there who no longer had his land. He still had plenty, he had a hacienda to live in.

I remember the dentist had this green Ford station wagon so he was able to drive us around and he took us to Mitla, which is an underground tomb cut from huge stone blocks. So little of that stuff remains. I wondered, where did that come from and how did they get that stuff there? They were fitted together, not mortared. And then there was a huge Banyan tree. I have a postcard somewhere of that Banyan tree that about fifty people are in a circle around holding hands. It is that big. A huge tree. It was the only tree. It must have been a major water source, to support that tree because everything around it—there wasn't anything. There wasn't forest. So I don't know what the deal was with that, but Mitla is a place where there were tombs, and all that was left were these underground caverns with gigantic stone blocks fitted together.

Then we discovered, right outside of Oaxaca, Monte Alban. The dentist took us there and then we found that we could walk up there if we started early when it was cool or we could go into town and go into the market.

Richard had a red beard by that time and the people called him chivo, goat. He didn't do too well in Mexico because he drank a lot, but also, he couldn't talk to anybody. They were only nine Americans down there at that time. Our friends, and their daughter, and six other people.

There was one couple we would meet at the market and the guy would argue with the market women. One day, one of the women got so irritated by him that she cracked an egg over his head. That was unheard of, that they would do that to a tourista. I kind of got to listen in to the Tehuantepec women, and they apparently have, at least economically, a matriarchal society.

They collect and hold the wealth and wear it, mostly on their bodies. Really beautiful filigree earrings and bracelets with little pearls. Nothing really large, but really beautiful jewelry. And then the rest of the women were spread around in other villages and they wore a serape. They were navy/indigo with little white workings. I had a shawl like that for a long time.

There was a mixture of Mayans from the Yucatan, and you could see the Maya. You can see it in Hawaii, there are coffee workers that are from, if you ask, if you go up to them, ask them if they are from Oaxaca, they will laugh and say, well, yes. And they're from that area and have the Mayan very high cheekbones and very almond eyes, very distinct. It goes back thousands of years.

When we walked across the field from town to our house, as we often did, our sandals would become completely clogged with the red volcanic mud. It rained a lot and the corn just grew and grew. There were a number of beggars on the street that we got to know and there was a boy who was a member of the Union of Unsalaried Workers. Our mouths just dropped when we heard this. They had a night school for the kids who were beggars or who worked during the day selling something, gum, or selling trinkets of some kind. There wasn't much of anybody to sell something to at that time. Oaxaca was not a grown-up city. It was just a market town for the surrounding villages. The people from those surrounding towns, like Ixtlan, would walk in ten, twenty miles the night before and camp there. Actually, they would come in on Thursday and leave on Sunday.

It was a market for people to exchange goods. Compared to the market in Mexico City, which was almost a half mile long, and a big concrete building. The market in Oaxaca was like Makuu Market, [a weekly market of about an acre in size near Pahoa, Hawaii].

The only other North Americans I remember were John and Claudia, their baby, she was about four. We used to sit in the plaza and drink beer, talk, have food, whatever, and there was a state militia in well-ironed but shabby uniforms and no weapons but every now and then the *Federales* would squeak in and everybody would disappear. I remember that happening several times. They would be looking for someone. It was pretty tense when the *Federales* came in. The other ones, the state police, were young boys. They got maybe a few *pesos*, they got a uniform to wear, and they carried lanterns, not even flashlights, just lanterns at night. They were there to keep order but the *Federales* were very different.

We were down there about three months. And probably too long. I think Richard got really bored and very depressed. I spoke Spanish pretty well, although I didn't have anything to talk to people about, really. You could always talk about the children or you could talk about food. He wrote constantly while we were there.

We started taking trips up to Monte Alban. There was a caretaker there, two or three. I don't think they worked for more than a few pennies a day. They showed us the stelae that were around the edges of this courtyard. At one end there was one temple and at the other end there was another temple. In the center, there was a structure where you could see the sun come through. We finally figured out it was some kind of an observatory to keep track of the seasons by the way the sun came through this slanted window. I've seen pictures of it. It's not much different now. They've done more excavation.

One day, we decided to climb up the mountainside and not go up by the road and we almost killed ourselves. So hot and so steep. We never did that again.

Later, in Mexico City, on the way out, we went to the museum and saw a lot of the artifacts that had been carted away from Oaxaca. At one time there had been a tremendous amount of gold and a lot of ornaments. There was a huge temple, probably several hundred priests lived there. It's up on a cinder cone, up about 500 feet from the valley floor. Maybe more than that. The valley floor was maybe a lake at one time. It's hard to tell, or maybe it was always just cornfields. But when you got up there, you could see the town of Oaxaca and then you then could see cornfields, and cornfields, and cornfields.

At that time, people still wore white pants and white tops out of cotton. They didn't so much wear shirts and jeans. Some did. The women wore their pupleles. They had the babies wrapped in them and they had their hair coiled on top. Some of them carried stuff on their heads. There were still intact pieces of culture.

One day, we walked up to Ixtlan and they were still re-building a church there, and gilding a carved altar piece with gold. Of course none of the people had shoes. They had sandals, but there were no vehicles. They were pretty well-fed; their teeth were in good shape. It was poverty. There were beggars. People weren't really suffering. There was a hospital and of course our friends were there for people without money.

There were mostly cafés. There wasn't a bookstore. There were bureaucratic offices. I don't know what those people did.

So, we stayed until our lease on the house was up. Then, we took a bus back to Mexico City, and had no particular adventures there, and a then bus to the border. We crossed at Nogales and hitchhiked back to L.A. and took a bus to San Francisco.

Coming back, we got stuck just over the border. It was 114 degrees [Fahrenheit]. It was just terrible, terrible hot. I have dark hair so I can't be in the sun that long. I'd come in and throw water on my head and we'd run back out and put our thumbs out. It took us about four or five hours to get a ride that time. That was the worst hitchhike I've ever had, because I thought I was going to die of heat stroke.

Then we got back to San Francisco and we decided that we would have a baby and that became the Adele Davis, *Eat Right To Keep Fit,* era: preparing for a pregnancy.

I think John was a writer, but then, in my memory, the word carpenter comes up, too. We didn't meet anybody in Mexico. If we had known where to meet people in Mexico, then I suppose we could have. We spent our time looking for paintings, Rivera, movies, looking at all the gold taken from the Aztecs, what survived. We didn't know anything about not only Mexican culture but Aztecan culture, their music or anything. We just didn't know. We weren't there long enough.

Oaxaca was beautiful. It was really beautiful.

One time, I found this fabric. It looked like it was hand-woven. It wasn't. It was really cheap. It was about ten cents a yard or something. So I bought several yards and we were going to go to an opera in Mexico City. God knows what that was about, but we were going to go to an opera. I don't even think it was the Ballet Folklorico. But we were going to go to some opera event, so I made this dress out of this stuff and when I showed up. It was either a restaurant or it was outside of the opera house. People were laughing and pointing at me. Not everybody, and they said, this woman is dressed *desire de derga*. I didn't know what they meant. It turned out that that fabric was what they made mops out of. I saw it later. They would fold over, a yard or so of this, and clamp it under the mop head for those spring mop heads.

So, I went to the opera in this dress that I thought was beautiful with a little thin stripe in it and it looked like it was hand-woven, it wasn't, I knew it wasn't, but really pretty. Only ten cents a yard. So my whole dress, my labor and all cost me three dollars, and I thought I was really smart.

Nobody ever laughed, after that, outside of Mexico City. It was people who recognized the fabric maybe from their village or their childhood, or their servants having used it. Nobody else laughed. They understood that I thought it was an inexpensive and beautiful fabric.

Richard kept turning out poems.

I realized it was time to go. One night he smashed a brandy glass against a wall. Not against me, he wasn't angry at me at that time. He had enough. He was just really depressed. He didn't want to stay any more.

You know how when you think in advance how long you're going to stay in a place and it turns out you really don't like it? You're stuck because you've already paid rent there.

We were about five miles out of town and the people, they couldn't figure out (it wasn't even the village, it was the suburbs, really) what the hell we were doing there. We didn't have any money. We weren't rich writers. We were just kids, you know. They weren't very friendly to us. We got the house because of this dentist and his connections to Don Luis Sarmiento who still had a few houses. That's how we got it. But then, a caretaker at Monte Alban, who we got to be really friendly with, taught us a tremendous amount about that site.

I remember examining these big stone carvings that were set upside down. I asked why they were upside down. The caretaker said that they were upside down because that's how they showed that they conquered their enemy. They would make the carvings and they would put them upside down. I don't know if that's true or not, but there were a lot of them. I suppose the reason they built the temple and the thing up top was because it was 600 feet above and you could see your enemies coming and you could repulse them.

In the center of that courtyard there was a ball court with a small circle. It wasn't more than fifteen inches around on the outside and the inside hole was a lot smaller. It was a stone circle up high and that was how they would hit it in with their hip. I don't know how they know this, but I've read this, that the game was like soccer but you hit the ball with your hip or maybe with your head. It took a tremendous amount of skill and stamina. That was their play. Now, whether the priests just stood around and watched people do that—or bet on it—who knows. Or, if the priests themselves were the players? I don't know. It's just some of the unknown stuff.

There was nothing at the ruins. They weren't overgrown. They had cleared away all the vegetation. It was dusty and hot. That was one of the things that made it hard to be up there if you didn't get up there in the morning. Baked. You'd get really hot and uncomfortable.

So, we'd got so we'd go late in the afternoon. If you went late in the afternoon, you didn't need the caretaker. If you went early in the morning, he'd give us a lecture, a tour. It was an adventure.

Nobody had discovered that. There were no buses churning up that road. Now there are. Oaxaca has probably a million people.

Some of the things survived. The Tehuantepec women wore gold jewelry and also wore these not hand-embroidered, but machine-embroidered white blouses with brilliant flowers on them and they still do that and they still sell them.

The dark side of Oaxaca was the mescal in these little black pots. I think it's the drunkest I have ever gotten in my life. Richard got into it pretty bad. There were these bars along the back streets of Oaxaca that just had a *pissoire* along the wall. There was this trough and the men would be drinking and they'd just turn and piss into that trough. There were people that stayed there all day, all night, all day, all night. It was really weird. It was like a skid row. I only looked in: no women.

That was another thing, walking around with Richard. He was conspicuous enough, but for a woman to be even looking in those bars was a no-no. No one did anything to me or to him because the people were basically afraid and basically kind. They tolerated our curiosity and they wanted more money than we had but if we didn't have it, they would take friendship instead. That what was really nice about Mexico at that time. I can't imagine now. The drug wars, the people going around with machine guns. I can't imagine.

I was really glad to get back to the United States despite of my love of Mexico, being able to speak the language, and all that, I was really happy. I guess I never really associated the fragility of a democratic society.

When we got back, Richard wrote *Please Plant this Book*.

The Reply of Trout Fishing in America:

There was nothing I could do. I couldn't change a flight of stairs into a creek. The boy walked back to where he came from.

The same thing once happened to me. I remember mistaking an old woman for a trout stream in Vermont, and I had to beg her pardon.

"Excuse me," I said. "I thought you were a trout stream. "
"I'm not," she said.

  —Richard Brautigan

Please Plant This Book
by Richard Brautigan

SWEET ALYSSUM ROYAL CARPET

I've decided to live in a world where
books are changed into thousands of
gardens with children playing
in the gardens and learning the gen-
tle ways of green growing things.

CALIFORNIA NATIVE FLOWERS

In this spring of 1968 with the last
third of the Twentieth Century
travelling like a dream toward its
end, it is time to plant books,
to pass them into the ground, so that
flowers and vegetables may grow
from these pages.

PARSLEY

I thank the energy, the gods and the
theater of history that brought
us here to this very moment with
this book in our hands, calling
like a future down a green and
starry hall.

SQUASH

The time is right to mix sentences
sentences with dirt and the sun
with punctuation and the rain with
verbs, and for worms to pass
through question marks, and the
stars to shine down on budding
nouns, and the dew to form on
paragraphs.

CALENDULA

My friends worry and they tell me
about it. They talk of the world
ending, of darkness and disaster.
I always listen gently, and then
say: No, it's not going to end. This
is only a beginning, as this book
is only a beginning.

CARROTS

I think the spring of 1968 is a good
time to look into our blood and
see where our hearts are flowing
as these flowers and vegetables
will look into their hearts every day
and see the sun reflecting like a
great mirror their desire to live
and be beautiful.

LETTUCE

The only hope we have is our
children and the seeds we give them
and the gardens we plant together.

SHASTA DAISY

I pray that in thirty-two years
passing that flowers and vegetables
will water the Twenty-First Cen-
tury with their voices telling that
they were once a book turned by
loving hands into life.

Camping

I grew up camping a lot. In those days, if you were a hundred miles out of L.A., in Mojave, for example, you were in the mountains.

My father was a fisherman, he liked to fish. He was one of five children. My mother was a school teacher and the youngest of eleven children. It took her sixteen summers to get her teaching license.

With Richard, we took two trips. We had an Indian theme going with Ianthe laced into a papoose board. We almost suffocated Ianthe, wrapping her up like that and we abandoned the idea.

It was some misguided Indian thing. We were gone two weeks to the Klamath River. Ianthe was too hot. When we took her out [of the cradleboard] she sort of unwrapped herself and threw a fit.

Later, on our trip across the Snake River we had a pink fabric leash [harness] that we tied to a tree. We used it one time because we were very close to the river. It had a steep cliff. A sharp drop-off to the river.

We almost didn't make it to Idaho. The first night, we drove down into an old lakebed—I think it was called Dollar Lake. Anyway, we had boxes in our 1951 Plymouth, books, boxes of clothing in the back of the station wagon in wooden crates, paper bags, baby stuff. Lots of Dostoyevsky, we couldn't go without Dostoyevsky! God forbid we go without that!

That night we slept inside the back of the car, everything was on the ground. Then, within minutes, a huge cloud burst. There was going to be a flood of mud, huge raindrops, dollar sized, the area began filling with water. I put Ianthe somewhere safe. I started driving up this road and I couldn't see.

We were in the middle of a huge cloudburst, we were almost stuck. The road wound around and around. It was so impossible to see. That was the first or second night of the trip.

That was the beginning of *Trout Fishing In America*.

Sleeping in the back of that station wagon. That's why it was so crazy. It was a shift car with the shift on the wheel.

Richard ate a lot of watermelon and had to pee in the night. That's why we were awake when the storm hit and found out the lakebed was filling in.

I don't know why we did the trip. Re-visiting Idaho, I guess. We saw the Snake River in the beginning of its decline and urban development.

It was Indian-based.

We were ahead or behind the times. Having a child was unusual at the time. There were some. Well, some had children. David and Tina Melzer had three kids. Ron Loewinsohn had a child later. Robert Creeley had children. But from what I read of Kerouac, his trips were not family-oriented.

It was quite amazing. The clutter of the station wagon. Now, there are containers for everything. There weren't then. Wooden crates and paper bags. A fabric tent.

We had a ridiculous tent. Stakes for the tent, food. The tent had to have stakes. It was canvas. It did not pop up. If a stake was lost, you had to find a tree, cut a new one.

We were re-enacting a whole bunch of stuff—it was a long trip. A canvas tent during the day is hot. Washing diapers in the streams—we weren't conscious of the fact that it was polluting.

We were usually the only people except for local fishermen. We saw some sheep, sheep farmers, and had to go through the herd of sheep and then came back round again, the sheep men just smiled. They knew [we weren't getting anywhere]. Richard wrote about this.

There were no maps, no guides; we went up and down the creeks until we found a good place.

We had travelers' checks and finding a place to cash them was hard. There was nowhere to cash them. Like in those novels where you read about the South, very backwoods. It wasn't convenient. Because we had gone to Mexico, to Oaxaca and had travelers' checks there, that might've been the reason we had them. Richard was paranoid about losing money.

Our baby was always an icebreaker. Richard had a song he sung, "Orofino Rose." He sang that over and over to Ianthe to get her to sleep.

Since I was raised in the San Fernando Valley, (it doesn't exactly inspire your imagination there), that was what I knew. San Francisco was really inexpensive when we lived there. It was a city with lots of culture, lots of poetry, but then, on the other hand, taking the trip was a break.

Richard was always writing. He sat at a card table with his Royal typewriter during the trip. I didn't know what he was writing until later. He was always taking notes. His short paragraphs were like poems. Real different writing. Coming back [after the trip], he was very short on words, not prolific, he wrote short chapters that were almost poems. They were so funny.

But everything changed. Ianthe was four when I met Tony (my later lover). Richard had become so abusive from alcohol. What boys see done to women in their youth…Richard and I weren't about that at all, we were into Camus—not towards others, but how we viewed ourselves.

Richard was fascinated by war—by WWI and WWII. He shot up one wall of his house in Montana which had a clock on it.

It was like a war, the sound of war. I didn't mind him going shooting, but we had this spaghetti party and he yanked the door open, afterwards. He didn't wake Ianthe, but he was very violent. I left soon after with Tony.

In Richard's poem, "All Watched Over By Machines Of Loving Grace," his writing is a predilection in a way, it has come true. There isn't anything you can do—the ether is full of good deeds and misdeeds—it all gets recorded. I've never looked back; I don't sit around and reflect on the past, I'm in the moment, in the now. I've lived that way my whole life.

People were living in communes and trying to be peaceful. What it came down to was falling into prior patterns. Richard just fell into that as far as I could see.

He liked Katherine Ann Porter a lot and also Eudora Welty. I think he had a special admiration for writers who were profound and humorous at the same time. He really liked the Armenian short story writer [Saroyan] who wrote, My *Name is Aram*. There were so many things that I didn't ask Richard about. It was us against the world and rebellion. Like living in a bubble. What did we want?

Freedom from the society that had jammed people into unhappy relationships and war. Freedom from that.

He created his own Kool-Aid reality and was able to illuminate himself by it.

—Richard Brautigan

Hawaii

I went back to school while I was working at the Women's Center of the Y.W.C.A. in Hilo.

That was an invented program, because the County of Hawaii gave up what were called C.E.T.A. jobs. I don't know what the acronym stood for. They weren't very high paying but we negotiated all those contracts—took them away from the county and founded a women's center at the Y.W.C.A. The director of the Y was astounded, she but she handled it very well. We didn't have enough space for offices, but a lot of new positions were outreach. Some of them were in Kona, one was in Waimea, we even had an outreach women's center in Kau. So we made good use of those jobs and they were extended, so it was about two and a half years. During that time I decided that I should get my degree. I asked the [Y.W.C.A.] director if I could start back to school and trade out because we often had events on Saturdays. We were there until five-six in the afternoon, we had groups in the evening; there were a million ways I could have made up the hours. Flex time was just not known. And she said that her board said no.

So I did it anyway.

We, I mean, I just flipped out, went to my classes in the afternoon. I could run up to the university, nobody knew that I wasn't doing the presentation on the Women's Center. It made me feel guilty, but not overly so. I was working sixty hours anyway for this project. I mean, I was really working hard to make a Women's Center a reality on the Big Island. We had an alternative job project; we had "displaced homemakers" which turned into a support group for divorcing and divorced women. Out of that came a shelter for battered women. And I worked there later for a time doing support groups. I started back to school and they looked at all my transcripts from U.C.L.A. and Santa Monica City College and Margaret Ushijima, a senator's wife, was the admissions director, and she sent a letter saying they'd admit me as a sophomore and I thought, no way, so I went back over there and I spoke to Margaret and I said, you know, Mrs.—Ms. Ushijima—I don't think we were using Ms. at that time—I said you know, I really think these credits are worth more than that. And some of them, I really did get good grades in. Some of them I totally didn't, and she laughed and then she put her hand up and beckoned to the back room and said, "Winnie!" to her assistant, and she just scribbled a few words on the papers and they admitted me as a junior.

So I needed only two years to finish. I stayed with political science and at the same time, I met Noelie Rodriguez and Jeff Crane, two professors in the sociology department. I had a dual major and got my B.A. in both those subjects, sociology and political science (master's degree at age 62-63).

So then, Women's Center jobs all folded and through another friend, a psychologist, Lee Sisson, who died about fifteen years ago of breast cancer, I heard about an opening in the state system for people with disabilities. For eleven years, I was the program specialist, the only person on the Big Island in charge of information and programs for people with disabilities. I travelled all around demonstrating how to make places accessible, explaining how they really needed to be and catching county and state projects before they were constructed so that they would include features to make them accessible.

In 1990 the Americans with Disabilities Act passed, and state legislation made it mandatory for review of these projects so I would get the O.E.Q.C. [Office of Environmental Quality Control] bulletin which would give advance notice of projects. I went to the architects, and begged them to send the plans to Honolulu for review, because it was free. They just needed to send their plans to the state, and specially trained architects would review them and show them how to do the doorways and ramps and other things that they hadn't thought about.

And so for eleven years I did that. It was a good job. I was totally my own boss, I was totally—had total integrity—and again, I said, I would like to go back to school to study for a master's degree and the answer came back, no. So I did it anyway.

It was the only thing, really, that I lied about, you know.

Now, the ironic thing was—I needed flex time. And I often did flex time anyway, going in on a Saturday, because there was a health fair or something where the Commission on Persons with Disabilities should be represented—and I would just do that. So it wasn't like I was cheating. Much later, in Honolulu, one of the program specialists became pregnant and all of a sudden, it was, Judy's baby, Judy's baby, Judy's baby.

And then it was *Judy's on flex time*—oh really? And then the director's mother got very ill. The director didn't have children, but she got flex time so she could take care of her mother. And I thought well, ha ha you guys, here I have four kids, never even breathed a word about flex time, hardly took a day off because I was never sick and then asked to do this educational advance and you said no. I mean, it was so bizarre.

So in '91, I was eligible to retire from the state (either in '91 or '93) and I switched over to the private sector. I got a really interesting job with the Papaya Commission. I met the papaya farmers who were almost all Filipino. That was in the middle of the G.M.O. [Genetically Modified Organism] controversy. Mostly, what I did was just write reports and minutes and did what they told me to do. We watched the G.M.O. people and Cornell University just gradually steal into the University of Hawaii agriculture system and introduce G.M.O. at the legislative level and begin planting genetically modified papaya.

They stopped ring spot virus to a certain degree but it made the papayas very vulnerable, it created a very short shelf life, and vulnerable to a rot around the blossom end. Now, even though they are marketing papayas again, they are small, half the size and have shorter shelf life than before.

I did all this with four kids.

I moved to Hawaiian Beaches, and bought a home.

I used to say I moved to Hawaii because of not having to match up socks and find winter jackets.

Tony, the kids' father, was on Oahu building a boat. That was his thing; he was going to go around the world. We were not together as a couple, but I decided to come to Hawaii—that was a whole section of my life. That was in 1976. I sold everything on the mainland, had a huge garage sale. Ianthe was with her father in Montana. Mara and Ellen were already in Hawaii with their dad, Tony. So Jesse, my son and I, got on a plane. We all lived in Ala Wai Harbor, on a boat, for about three months. But the boat wasn't sailing. Then I met a doctor from the university who wanted to go solo sailing. He was content to have me come along to fix a few meals and operate the emergency radio if that became necessary. He really didn't want me to set the sails.

He was practicing for solo sailing. So I thought, well, that's about as good as it gets.

So I took Mara and Jesse and we sailed all around Hawaii. We sailed to Maui and back. We sailed to Lanai and back, we sailed to Molokai and back and we sailed to Maui and back again and then around Oahu over a period of six months. So not all instantly. One problem was he kept trying to get me in bed with him and he was a married person. His wife wouldn't go sailing with him. He needed a sailing partner, but he wanted a lot more than that.

He said he wanted to do solo sailing but I've often wondered if he ever did that, or if that was just a ploy to get me on the boat.

It was an incredible adventure, but after I got off the boat, I never did it again. I did not become a sailor. I didn't have the reflexes for it.

Yeah, really, well, everybody at the harbor—was really surprised—a lot of them had sailed but it was like in the past. They were really just living on boats because it was free rent. One woman was making shell necklaces. These became good friends and they also took care of my kids when I worked. We all worked occasionally ferrying rental cars back and forth from the harbor to the hotels. They paid cash and it was pretty exciting zipping through Honolulu traffic.

Tony was supposed to be taking care of the girls, Ellen and Mara; he and the women who lived there were terribly lackadaisical about the girls' care. I didn't know that until later. I don't know why I was so stupid about him. I just was. I was besotted, I guess I was in love for a long time. But when that was over, it was just over. It was me and my four kids on Oahu.

Ianthe came back from Montana, we moved to Kaneohe to this place across from Waiahole Valley. And Waiahole Valley was in turmoil because they wanted to put condos up at the top of it, just above the school. Mara and Jesse were going to that school. She had a terrible time. The local girls teased her. So I became an Avon representative and went up the valley and went to each house and introduced myself and my pretext was to give them the Avon book. I didn't sell much but I got to know the parents. And once I did that, the harassing stopped. Then, I did a lot of typing for George Helm and Walter Ritte who were holding sovereignty meetings on the lawn of the school. They were working on taking back Lanai.

A friend who was in the harbor and I got together and she said, let's go to the Big Island. I could see that there was very little way for me to make a living in Honolulu for myself with four kids—and so I just took a huge leap into the unknown and we got our airline tickets. She shipped her stuff over and her blue truck and we started looking for a place in Hilo. I don't know what she thought she was going to do, but there was a man involved for her and he sort of disappeared. He was a cane cutter, one of the top cane cutters, made the most money. It's a part of the cane process where you slice off pieces of the cane that they're going to plant. They put it in a growth solution and then plant it later. Going through the field and selecting those things and putting them into bundles is like a competition to see who could do the most. Anyway, he kind of turned out not to be there for her. She had two boys.

We met a realtor one rainy afternoon in Hilo, a Japanese-American woman. We didn't realize that ninety-nine percent of the realtors at the time, whether they were Japanese-American or not wouldn't have even looked at us—but she was trying to rehabilitate this house on Waimalino Lane in Wainaku and we offered to prep and paint the downstairs in exchange for the first two months' rent and the deposit and we lived in the upstairs. It was a beautiful house, gone now, torn down. Then my friend and her boys moved into the downstairs which was a lot more comfortable for everybody. The house was right by the Wainaku River and the kids went down there every day, and swam and played.

I just thought Hilo was a wonderful place, so I got a job as a VISTA Volunteer. I worked as a paralegal for Legal Aid for two years and that morphed into YWCA Women's Center. This is Hawaii's story, they start these great programs with federal dollars and then they can't afford to keep the people even after they're trained and doing a good job.

I wanted a new start and something different, that's why I went to Hawaii. Tony opened up the idea of living at the harbor and it sounded great, and it was great. It was really an amazing time. It reminded me of the time that I described when we lived in the Haight-Asbury because there was clothing that people would discard as they jumped on boats and went away, there was always fish. There was always a barbeque of some kind, and at that time the boats were tied up— little peanut boats— behind the big boats to avoid paying harbor fees. And of course Ala Wai Harbor was a mess, it was a stinking mess, you didn't dare drop anything or fall in.

It gets that way with too many people in too small an area. It's like the Sausalito house boat area. Periodically, they just have to clean it out.

There was a woman there who had a shark under her boat. Not a big one. She kept it in a rectangular, quite long, cage. The shark could turn around in it. She told me that was her *amakua*. That was really my introduction to anything about Hawaiian culture. And I understood what that was, you know. That wasn't a pet. That was her connection with her ancestors.

I've lived a long time in Hawaii now. Thirty years, thirty-five. I moved to Oahu in 1976.

I then moved to Hawaii Island in 1978 and worked for Legal Aid.

From 1978 to 1979 was the Women's Center era, and I got to travel. I went to Dallas for a women's conference, I went to Florida for a women's conference, there was all this money available to go and nobody wanted to do that. They didn't want to be openly feminist. There was just a group of maybe fifteen, twenty women, very diverse, but most of them either couldn't or didn't want to leave their families and do that kind of traveling.

And so, I would go. I still like traveling.

I ended up by being my own trout and eating the slice of bread myself.

—Richard Brautigan

Afterward

So many community meetings start with, "Tell us a little about yourself."

When that happens, I need to decide where to focus in describing my life. I feel I've lived four or five lifetimes already.

There are themes and cycles that I've gone through. I see that looking back. When looking back, I see my involvement in politics and I see that my life has simply gone in cycles. Most of the time it comes to money or votes, you stick your foot in that door if it opens a little and keep it in and say, create a skate park or a women's center, as I've helped to accomplish.

Where does this impetus originate in my life? This goes back to my Methodist Youth group that I attended when I was twelve years old. I realized that churches, in going to different countries and trying to help or become involved in humanitarian endeavors, are able to make some positive changes in communities.

My father also contributed to my sense of service or active involvement. He outfitted his sheepherders better than anyone else in our area with their supplies and their wagons. Before we moved to California, he paid off debts in Idaho. My brother conducted research and found a bunch of articles about his mediation efforts of water rights to the Snake River in the 1920's. So, I suppose I inherited a bit of feistiness from him, as well as a sense of scholarship from my grandmother.

When I was a young woman living in San Francisco, I remember wearing black turtlenecks and living in North Beach. Tour buses passed through town and someone was saying, "Look, at the Beatniks" as they passed by. We had a discussion going about that term back then. "Bohemian" was what we wanted to be referred by. It sounded more refined and elegant. This probably had something to do with the leisure class in Bohemia, in Europe, in Vienna.

Then, suddenly, everything was about the "Beat Generation" and this label soon became synonymous with being lackadaisical, and stoned-out because of drugs, acid, and dropping out of school and society. It was also about the music, the "beat" in music.

As far as the term, "fauxhemian," being applied to the Gen-Xers and younger, I would have to say that I'm living in the middle of it in Pahoa, Hawaii.

I went to see Janis Joplin in North Beach at The Place and remember being astounded by the passion and the atonality of the music. She seemed to be screaming her pain. I realized that pain was being expressed through music. I realized that it was also expressing the alienation from family and school that was a lot of peoples' experience. It wasn't until later that I realized how drugs and alcohol exaggerated the pain.

At that time most of the people I knew created little enclaves where they cooked exotic foods, for example, while trying to live as simply as they could. Later, the Haight Asbury became a haven for a collection of individuals seeking something that probably did not exist. It was common for poets in North Beach, with their love of the outdoors and love of nature to spend the weekends out hiking and swimming in the wilds. Some even moved out, such as Robert Creeley and his family when they left and moved to Bodega Bay.

Spend your time on the things that have the longest reach. This would be my advice to anyone. Spend that time towards the education of children and the humanization of children and also toward the preservation of the planet. These are worthwhile causes to which one should be devoted, in my opinion.

To writers or their muses seeking advice, whether they are young and beginning or seasoned, it comes down to the same thing: keep writing. Richard said, and it is a known saying, that what makes a good writer is about thirty years of writing. He was unable to follow his own advice. He followed his own sexual and physical yearnings. This is especially evident in his last novel. The dilemma he was faced with was this: what do I do if I can't seduce women anymore?

As far as my feelings about this book being published, I say this: everyone wants to feel validated and that they had something to add to human consciousness to help lift beyond the pain of everyday living. Some of the things that have happened to me are just so funny. I hope readers see the humor in my account of my past.

As I reached back in the past for stories of my life for this book, it was especially fun for me to relive the jokes people played on each other when they were young.

Notes on "A Boat" by Richard Brautigan:

This poem is about a friend, Lester Rosenthal, we had in San Francisco. We saw some werewolf movies and Lester came with us. Lester got so frightened during the movie that he hid under his theater seat and was howling in fear. We had to carry him out of the theater. It wasn't a joke. The movie had terrified our friend. It was a silent Lon Chaney film. We went through this thing where we saw silent films right when I first met him.

Notice in the Hawaii Tribune-Herald, 1980s.

American Association of University Women Puna Branch presents...

More... More... Encore!

WOMEN'S COMEDY '95

ALOHA THEATRE, Kainaliu
Saturday, October 21; 7:30 p.m.

Advance Tickets $8 --At The Door $10

Tickets available at:
Rhythm and Reading- Waimea, Kailua-Kona
Aloha Store (next to Aloha Theatre)
Keauhou Village Bookstore - Keauhou Shopping Center

AMERICAN
ASSOCIATION OF
UNIVERSITY
WOMEN

Tax deductible contribution to:
American Association of University Women
Educational Foundation, Phone: Ginny Aste 965-9869

Another run for State Representative, 1980s.

Skate park crew, 2000s. Gary Safarik (holding sign) backed the skate park in Pahoa during his tenure on the Hawaii County Council.

Blessing Ceremony, Ginny Aste Skate Park

Dinner In The Park crew, 1990s. Free dinner on Sunday afternoons for six years.

Campaign for State Representative, Green Party. 1980s.

"Domestic Harmony" campaign. This was an attempt to change the language of "domestic violence." 1980s-90s.

U.S.D.A. community garden in Pahoa, Hawaii, 1990s.

**2002
GOVERNOR'S KILOHANA AWARD
for
OUTSTANDING VOLUNTEERISM**

is hereby presented to

Virginia Aste

Your special acts of Aloha have enriched the lives of those around you. Mahalo!

Benjamin J. Cayetano
Governor, State of Hawaii

First skate park t-shirt, fundraising for the Pahoa Skate Park that was to become the Ginny Aste Skate Park in 2018. Colin Green, far left, Paradise Newland (in hat), Michael Hyson in Aloha shirt.

For Here: On Interviewing Virginia Brautigan Aste
by Susan Kay Anderson

"This whole idea of changing your own personal culture from place to place, time to time, and person to person shows that culture is indefinite, ever fluctuating, and at most, just a concept. Can there be a true sense of culture if people are unique and individual, and not just part of the group? Forests need to be seen for trees, not just the forest itself. It is often easier, however, to look past a person's individuality, and deny them said individuality, in order to just see a group."[1]

Who hasn't experienced the ho-hums, the doldrums of the new millennium and an inexplicable longing for simpler times? The 1950s? The 1960s? All of a sudden, it isn't a person who needs rehab, but the entire economy is in crisis (again) and nostalgia for simpler times, simpler ways abounds. Gardens are being scratched out of front lawns; people are hanging up their wash on lines. As an ex-pat of the frisky towns of Eugene, Oregon and Boulder, Colorado, my own life as a bohemian had been boiled down, diluted, and boiled down again by hanging out for stolen moments during my teen's soccer games at the local Starbucks, sipping a Pike's Place *for here* in a *for here* ceramic mug—you need to say it twice or the paper cup is already sitting in front of you with a plastic lid on it—and my gloomy musings about David Foster Wallace, newest casualty of the new writers, the hope of the hopefuls, who bled and then stopped his own airway, breathing, and circulation in one fell swoop. On Hawaii's Big Island, too far away from Dennis Suyeoka's Coffeeline in Lower Manoa Valley on Oahu, my bohemian dreams (despite living in Pahoa) seemed unreachable, intangible.

Then, a miracle happened at my job teaching at a "hard-to-staff/hard-to-fill" school. No, it wasn't a so-called breakthrough in educating large groups of belligerent teens, no, it wasn't that I was put on leave for sending a student to detention for dress code violation. It was most unexpected, as true miracles are; my substitute teacher told me she was married to bohemian Dadaist writer Richard Brautigan before he became

---

1. Cho, Alyssa; Schuber, Michael; Scott, Wayne, *In Spite of the Mainstream: Ideology of an Eatery* [Coffeeline], 2006, Anth. 200, Dr. Christine Yano, University of Hawaii-Manoa, ts.

known as a famous Beat Writer, a literary giant in the 60's and 70's with: *Trout Fishing In America, Revenge of the Lawn, Hawkline Monster, In Watermelon Sugar* and other precious packets of words. Have you ever been given a gift you don't quite know what to do with? That's the way I felt when I asked Virginia Brautigan Aste to be interviewed and she said yes, giving me some of her recollections about the life and times of this famous, troubled writer. My self-imposed status as fauxheminan could now be put on hold; vicariously, tentatively, indefinitely.

How to introduce Richard Brautigan's writing if one has never stumbled across his books nor had them on their parents' bookshelf while growing up?

My parents' groovy (read: younger) friends Stan and Susie, fresh out of college and living in the same government housing on the Walker River Indian reservation where we lived, gave Brautigan's books to my parents inadvertently when they stored stuff at our house. When we moved to Oregon, seemingly settled—Mom announced to (Dad apparently knew) my sisters and I that they were "having difficulties" and that she was "making some decisions." During that time, we had Richard Brautigan's books and my sister Tina and I read them. They really cheered us up because they were filled with so much ennui, just like our real lives were. *Trout Fishing In America* was so damn familiar. It was about the Pacific Northwest where we lived. All its grandeur and boredom. We got high just by reading. Tina and I knew kids just like the Kool Aid Wino. We were those kids. Our sister, Corine, was observed to be such a wino. We had spent many many hours fishing when we lived in Nome and camping out in the wild. We were reading about ourselves, reading our own thoughts. We were putting off going absolutely crazy.

Was it was possible to reach beyond the velvety plushness of my bohemian dreams and get glimpses into a simpler? past in the here and now by speaking with the someone who was there, right there, almost mothering the wonderful work of the wonderful life and times of Richard Brautigan—nurturing an enigma—nurturing his enigmatic writing that stood for the vastness, the quaint, the inexplicable West?

About 20 miles from the active vent of Hawaiian Volcano Kilauea, I interviewed Virginia Brautigan Aste about her first husband (they were married some ten odd years and mostly separated during these). Their daughter, Ianthe Brautigan Swenson, author of *You Can't Catch Death: A Daughter's Memoir* (St. Martin's Press, 2000) was born in 1960. Besides working as a substitute teacher in the public school system, Virginia is a political activist, having been recently affiliated with open space proponents, Puna Friends of the Park, running three times for State House of Representatives, and having been involved with sustainability planning, among other pursuits.

Virginia responded to my request for an interview, my questions, and to the waitress who took our breakfast orders at the Black Rock Cafe in Pahoa in a matter of fact, "of course" way. She is not a little old lady type, no, not this septuagenarian, she is almost six feet tall, wears wellfitting outfits and interesting jewelry, glasses, and short-cropped dark hair. Her gaze never wavers, she laughs easily and speaks in a slower, serious way, in a quiet tone. She is quite funny and self-effacing, able to laugh at herself, not in a hee-haw way, but in a measured, self-paced way. O.K., she doesn't strike one exactly as a librarian, but...she could be. That impression is probably due to the fact that I see her almost every time I go to the library in Pahoa, a teeny tiny spot of scholarly activity in the Ohia forest/jungle area of Puna, on Hawaii's Big Island. A place where a very generous patron regularly leaves old copies of the *London Times Book Review* at the free table, right next to pamphlets on how to prevent contracting the deadly rat lung disease from common garden snails.

To work as a substitute teacher in one of the most disadvantaged school districts in Hawaii is quite brave, to say the least. She comes across as a survivor, and also a people-person, but not overly so. Not that she's battle-worn and burnt-out, but Virgina Brautigan Aste seems a bit tired of the struggles she's experienced and has watched her family go through over the years. She spent a majority of them as a single mother of four and is now an active grandmother to her grandchildren.

Part Two

I meet with Virginia several more times in 2009 to continue the interview about Richard Brautigan. Previous to this, I remain out of my job, fall into a weird numbness, a depression, and avoid the interview, typing it up. I learn that Ianthe has ovarian cancer and has to undergo surgery and treatment. [She has since recovered]. It seems like a touchy time, inappropriate to dig around further into the past when the present is falling apart. My AIG retirement account is wiped out, my teaching placement for next year is questionable, and my daily job search at the local employment center is full of familiar faces from parts of routine life—getting my oil changed and weekend hiking up at the volcano. Tino, the top salesman from Mazda, and the guy who ran around Volcano House in the national park managing everything for the past twenty years have been laid-off and are also at the employment center. Then, Steve, the manager from Mazada is also running around there and also the top waiter from Volcano House.

When I finally meet with Virginia again, it's on Mother's Day. The week after that, Virginia is excited about the issue of *Sierra* magazine she came across, and in it, an article ("Baby On Board," Doug Fine, *Sierra*, May/June, 2009) chronicling a couple's journey with their infant down the Green River in Utah. She tells me that their trip reminded her of the infamous Idaho trip and that Ianthe was very small, too, like their son. "Lucky they had an umbrella," she said, "they just happened to bring one along and lucky they did because there was no shade."

What is the metaphor for the interview?

Interviewing Virginia is a bit like piling building blocks on top of each other or else it is kind of like she accesses a book that's already been written. She speaks completely—does not search and waver. Maybe I'm not asking her the difficult questions, the nosy ones.

Virginia Brautigan Aste speaks very plainly. She does not frill things out. Not really. Maybe it is in the absence of elaboration where her elaboration lies. Or else, this interview would be like crying or like an animal sound, grunts and callings instead of words. Calling for the past. Calling for mercy.

***

After completing the interview about Richard Brautigan, I looked at my notes from that time: we agree to begin what seems like a new project, interviews about Virginia and about her life.

Some of my notes:

Virginia is attending the first roller derby in Hilo tonight, because she's been, "interested in the skate parks"—developing the Pahoa Skate Park and now plans for a Hilo skate park are in the works. She's involved in creating a community kitchen.

She grew up listening to her dad's stories when he was a Marine in WWI. "He was a pilot and dropped bombs. They had to synchronize the gun and the propellers so the propellers didn't get shot off. The way he talked, he was the only one in the air. I imagine him with a long, white scarf flowing out of the airplane. He was 22 when his dad died. He never spoke of his dad, not at all, almost as if his dad was not there at all." I write that: *She is a very practical person. Very definitely a person who is scheming, thinking, planning, connecting constantly—on a constant basis. That's how it goes. Business contracts, keeping up, keeping track and moving and shaking.*

I learn that she is community-minded from years ago. It is not a new interest.

"Living in Bodega Bay and also Sonoma County—the most beautiful place was right inside that Redwood grove at Frobel School. They had to unpack school stuff for Monday through Thursday [classes]. Then, pack up again. Kids played Indians, crept through the marsh—no poison oak up at that altitude in the forest. There was music, art education, film making—all the early education stuff."

When she went to Utah a while back, she looked at some skate parks there.

"At different designs—one in Salt Lake and one in Logan, one in Brigham City. The one in Logan was a bit better than the one in Salt Lake."

She found the intellectuals, the thinkers and artists of the times wherever she was, she was attracted to them (they found her). Knowing her, interviewing, speaking to Virginia Brautigan Aste, has been lucky in the extreme, helping me to understand history, Brautigan and other writers, my own parents and myself, for getting a glimpse of the times, the attitudes and mores of the times, the language and humor and the struggle of the times—what was important then that has been lost? What is important now, looking back?

A book is supposed to take you places you've never been before. New ground new territory to another way of thinking, feeling. Characters that you get to know. *A Confederate General from Big Sur* and *Trout Fishing In America* did just that—introduced America to a new way of looking at the landscape—physical and cultural. Richard Brautigan's writing was filled with the weird characters and observations that were so strange; they were quite familiar, recognizable.

Virginia Bautigan Aste was someone who was there then, when the "there" kept shifting around. She was a fortuitous voyager who did not stop in her tracks, but ventured into the unknown with an unknown writer—Richard Brautigan—for a time—before venturing on. His second book sold three million copies, brought him instant fame, and secured his future writing career—every artist's dream come true. Did he accomplish this publishing miracle by himself? Virginia did not receive any recognition, revenue, or rights from his success.

This book is the result of interviews with Virginia Brautigan Aste from 2008 to 2015. We met in the Black Rock Cafe in Pahoa, Hawaii, for Florentine omelets and coffee. I would ask her about her life and she would speak into a tape recorder. We've continued our friendship and she made a trip to Oregon in 2019 to attend the Oregon Poetry Association's Fall Conference where we read parts of this book to attendees.

This book also introduces Virginia Brautigan Aste, known to her East Hawaii Island community as a substitute teacher, grant writer, community activist, single mother of four and grandmother, but known to the rest of the world as Richard Brautigan's first wife. Little has been written about her besides mentioning her in Brautigan biographies; the most extensive information is on a wikipedia page and on John F. Barber's Brautigan Archive site. So, this book is a coming out, as well. It is our hope that more Beat era women will write and speak about their lives; even if they are seemingly overshadowed by their partner in terms of success or fame.

This is what I've found interviewing Virginia Brautigan Aste: extreme humility, patience, lots of laughter, a dash of hesitation, a natural narrative style during our sessions, and a huge generosity in sharing her experiences, opinions and views.

Most people are aware of the Beat legacy and its influence on writing, culture, music, and art. Recent books documenting women's detailed involvement: *Off The Road,* by Carolyn Cassaday, *Minor Characters: A Beat Memoir,* by Joyce Johnson, *Use My Name: Jack Kerouac's Forgotten Families,* by Jim Jones, *You'll Be O.K., My Life With Jack Kerouac,* by Edie Kerouac-Parker, *Just Kids,* by Patti Smith, *Women of the Beat Generation,* by Brenda Knight, Diane di Prima's *Recollections of My Life as a Woman & Memoirs of a Beatnik,* and *Beats at Naropa* by Anne Waldman. Poet Tom Clark's extensive biographies have added excellent research to the body of knowledge about the Beats.

Brautigan gives us hints that specific women acted as muse because he featured them on the covers of his books. There was one woman missing from these book covers—Virginia Brautigan Aste. Also missing is her story and what shaped her personality in terms of experiences and people—and how she met, married, and supported the struggling writer that was her husband.

She was the one who provided the main income, wheels, typewriter, and ability to connect with others that R.B. may have lacked at the beginning of his career. She was a savvy Californian, after all. He was an Oregonian—from a small college town surrounded by the woodsy out-of-doors. They both were poor and together (young) traveled around as only the rich generations had before. It was the 1960's and they were part of the wave of change, right smack in the middle of it, just like thousands of other young Americans, only, they brought that view into the landscape and geography of the Pacific Northwest and looked at that familiar place in a new way.

Trout Fishing In America touched hearts, evoked hilarity, and changed the imaginations of readers and writers forever. It would not have been possible without Richard Brautigan's first wife, Virginia, who hauled the typewriter home from work every evening on the bus in order to help him type up his poems. This was a young, struggling couple—an artist trying to produce work, have the stable family that he never had, and contend with being supported by a resourceful, educated, energetic, and very practical wife who was extremely curious, had a rebellious streak, and was the ultimate Bohemian. They had a darling daughter that they both doted on, probably spoiled, and nurtured like the tender yet resilient plant that she was. She made their lives extremely difficult but extremely interesting because she was the baby. They were forced to grow up in a time and place that was becoming increasingly unraveled. Nothing went according to their wishes—everything and everyone was changing so rapidly around them-especially themselves. Alcohol exaggerated their challenges.

In the poem, "A Boat," by Richard Brautigan, a werewolf cries as he apparently drowns. In an interpretation of this image, poet and Beat biographer Tom Clark offers the following [*Tom Clark/Beyond The Pale*, online, comments section, December 25, 2011],

"No one can help him. The carnival only makes things worse. The bright lights trick the tears into visibility. Out on the dark waters of the Bay, it might almost be possible to sink unnoticed."

We as readers are not really supposed to help or feel sorry for him but see this creature, Clark cautions as,

"Difficult keeping afloat anyway, in that tub of industrial crud... but what you can't see can't hurt you until you smell & feel it... wept the bewildered werewolf to himself, just as the spot lights caught him from above, not waving but drowning."

Virginia Brautigan Aste was someone who did not sink, drown, or otherwise disappear and here you will find out what happened in her life.

Escaping with Ianthe was much like the disappearing of the last of the Romanoff in the Russian Revolution, Virginia got the hell out of Dodge and fled to Utah with her new lover, Tony. This book is about a woman who mixed and mingled with artists and writers at the time of America's great change in consciousness—the 1960's.

We can look back at the Bohemians to find out what to do now—how to live, eat, breathe—to guide us forward in the face of rapid change. Their innocence is beguiling. The monsters of addiction got a hold of many after biting them. This is the story of one woman who witnessed both—from the beginning of her life in Idaho, growing up with a fantastic dreamer of a father who dictated her life, Virginia broke away and studied at U.C.L.A. and Santa Monica City College, moved to New York, and worked and then moved to San Francisco, gathering a lot of experiences in the changing cultural climate before meeting and marrying Richard Brautigan.

This book tries not to be about Richard Brautigan but how can it not be about him, or in reference to him? Virginia remains guilty by association. Every move she's done before or since meeting him could be read as somehow related to Richard Brautigan and his movements/writings/whereabouts. She was definitely on her own life path; collided with Brautigan, lived life to the fullest and then saw the time to make a break for it before being consumed. She then kept going—living briefly in Utah and then back to San Francisco with Tony Aste and having children and eventually settling down on the Big Island of Hawaii. She was extremely inventive, very resourceful, and therefore did not drown.

From Virginia Brautigan Aste's College Papers: "Dear Noelie"

"Dear Noelie"

This is a six page paper written for Dr. Noelie Rodriquez' Sociology 100 course at the University of Hawaii, Hilo, Hawaii, in 1984. Virginia states that she "will turn fifty in July" of 1984. This paper is written in the first-person, epistolary form. Her professor writes very enthusiastic comments at the end of the paper. Virginia's writing is detailed and precise. It is interesting that she states:

"My mother and father were both teachers in their teen years and I learned to read early, skipping a grade, which allowed me to graduate from high school when I was 15. I then went to UCLA (1951-55) where I became enmeshed in the daily paper and political sciences courses, but did not graduate.

My father was an alcoholic and a source of embarrassment and frustration to me in my teen years. I left home primarily because of his constant criticism and insanity."

Virginia goes on to say, "I won essay contests and public speaking was always easy for me."

Toward the end of this essay, she writes this:

"I have always put a tremendous value on learning for its own sake. I believe that our survival on earth is in jeopardy and have always looked for ways to create good and share them, encourage individuality and equality between children and adults, and wondered at the blindness of people who cannot see what they are doing to the planet in the name of progress. I have begun to realize that much of the destruction is perpetuated by men, not women."

Virginia Aste
Sociology 100
Dr. Rodriguez

Dear Noelie:

In July 1984, I will be fifty years old.

I spent 18 years of my life in the San Fernando Valley in a town called Reseda, which at that time had 2,500 inhabitants and a hitching post outside the post office. I attended grammar school in Reseda and went to high school in Canoga Park, a town two miles west with even fewer people. Canoga Park was an agricultural center and there was a Hispanic population, resident and migrant which gave me my first awareness of cultural difference and discrimination.

My mother and father worked and lived in the town and I have a younger brother who now lives with his family in Lake Arrowhead. My mother was outgoing and loving, sang in the choir and worked in a grocery store from the time I was six or seven years old. My brother and I and a cousin my same age stayed across the street from my house with my aunt and grandmother.

My identification with my grandmother has always been strong. She was a German immigrant who lived and worked on a farm all her life until one of her three sons brought her to California to live on the "1/2 acre in paradise," that he bought with proceeds from the sale of the Nebraska farm.

My mother and father were both teachers in their teen years and I learned to read early, skipping a grade, which allowed me to graduate from high school when I was 15. I then went to UCLA (1951-1955) where I became enmeshed in the daily paper and political science courses, but did not graduate.

My father was an alcoholic and a source of embarrassment and frustration to me in my teen years. I left home primarily because of his constant criticism and insanity.

-1-

Early in my life I had asthma, which set me apart from other kids somewhat and directed me to the library rather than athletic games. I was always more interested in reading and writing than playing games, although I remember tag football and winning letters in volleyball and baseball.

I won essay contests and public speaking was always easy for me.

When I attended college, I learned about the holocaust and became acquainted with Jewish culture through my roommate and a group of women who formed an off-campus living center which was the only cheap place to live and certainly counter-culture to the sororities!

There were no women professors at UCLA ~~at that~~ time except in the education department and perhaps the music department. *[margin: Actually, I (almost 4 now) also had the lack of role model situat-]* I never knew a woman doctor, lawyer or business owner, most of my friends were married immediately after high school,(some before) and had one, two or three children by the time I was in my sophomore year. Birth control, sex and sexuality were not talked about, although I *became* sexually active and was fitted for a diaphraghm after getting ~~VD~~ and not knowing for a week what it was.

I left Southern California and went to New York in 1956 where I met a 65 year old radical who introduced me to classical music, health foods, art and politics, although we had many arguments because he was a Stalinist. His energy was appalling, we rode bikes and walked everywhere, talking incessëntly.

We parted when I left for San Francisco, intending to return to school. Instead I met a poet and entered the beatnik era *[margin: I did this]* in S.F., with poetry readings, endless philosophical discussions

-2-

The poet?

and eventually Richard (Brautigan) and I decided to have a child. I attended Lamaze classes and read everything I could get my hands on about child-raising and child development. It wasn't much help. I was 26, and the pictures of me with Ianthe the first few weeks after she was born make me wonder how I survived. She was a marvelous child, taken on many camping trips and I taught her to read when she was about four years old. She is now 24 and lives in New York with her husband of two years.

I spent the next twelve years with Tony Aste, and have three children as a result of that union. Ellen was born five years after we met, Ianthe was 8 years old and we had Ellen at home with Tony as "midwife". That birth was a wonderful experience and I have always felt a special closeness to Ellen as a result.

Mara was born three years later and we intended a home birth, but it became difficult, a little frightening, and we went to the hospital. I became pregnant again and had Jesse, my last child and a boy, at a small hospital in Sonoma, California. Ellen and Mara were both born in San Francisco. By that time we lived in the country for good, we thought.

Tony had an accident in which he almost lost his leg and after that, seemed unable to cope with raising or even parenting his children. He came and left and each time I became stronger and more determined to survive on my own. I still feel betrayed because of the financial abandonment, but we had many good trips together -- to Mexico, to Salt Lake City, to Northern California and he certainly taught me survival skills.

When Ellen and Mara were small 5, 6, years old, Tony took them to Hawaii and to Guam, where they learned to sail and learned to love Hawaii. I brought Jesse and Ianthe and we moved to the Big Island about eight years ago.

I worked as a secretary most of the time I was in school, at various part time jobs. When I went to New York, I sought work in publishing, but got sidetracked in several others things, taking classes at Columbia University in drama and Greek and working in an office there, later managing a mosaic shop and learning to copy music. When I came to San Francisco, I landed a temporary job in a law firm and learned to be a legal secretary. I returned to work when Ianthe was five months old. I worked prior to Ellen's birth in a secretarial service, went on part time when she was two months old and back to full time soon after. It never occurred to me to think of work as a career. My career was my children.

Because of my dislike and distrust of public schools, I was involved in starting a school in S.F. There were about 24 kids, extremely varied in development, background and age, but the group process and the opportunity to be there with my two older girls and Mara when she was about six weeks, was a valuable, exciting experience. I had earlier started a nursery school in North Beach.

When we moved to the country (Sonoma County) I started a nursery school at my home with six other mothers, and two years later about 25 families started an elementary school which is still in operation. I began receiving welfare help and was able to combine volunteering at the school with home sales and lived fairly comfortably -- utilities paid and a car and phone.

-4-

Sonoma County was wonderful as a place to raise children. We lived on two different "farms" -- places which had been farms and which could accomodate chickens, a garden, a horse, a giant dog or two and which had trees and fields and creeks to explore. Town was only a couple of miles away and trading food and child care and clothing was easy.

Before I left Sonoma, I began to be aware of the conflict between my brain and my uterus, and to wonder what I could and would do to support myself and my family. I realized that I had never allowed myself to wonder why I had children -- although I maintained until fairly recently that I "chose" to have them. I certainly never speculated before I had children whether or not I would have them -- it was a given. It is only recently that I can see I might never have considered having children if I had thought that was an acceptable choice.

I have always put tremendous value on learning for its own sake. I believe that our survival on earth is in jeopardy and have always looked for ways to create goods and share them, <u>encourage individuality and equality between children and adults</u>, and wondered at the blindness of people who cannot see what they are doing <u>to the planet in the name of progress</u>. I have begun to realize that much of the destruction is perpetrated by men, not women. *I AGREE*.

Since coming to Hawaii, I learned to be a paralegal assistant and worked with indigent people, doing hearings for restoring benefits -- food stamps, shelter costs, unemployment benefits, social security. <u>I was a co-founder of the Women's Center, the Family Crisis Shelter, the Sexual Assault Support Service</u> and wrote many of the grants as well as the programs.

A year and a half ago, I returned to school (after 23 years) and am now finishing the last three units of a B.A. degree in political science. I don't find that things have changed all that much. Imperialism in Latin America was very much the same, although the US involvement was not as apparent, in 1955. Development in Africa has exploded, but that is not a specialty of the department here. I became interested in sociology after taking a course in hermeneutics from Jeff Crane and have decided that I will study for a second B.A. during the next year.

Through the women's movement, which was just beginning to be powerful when I left the mainland, I have gained insights about my own life, the universality of poverty for women and the strength of collective power. Money (or lack of it) is an ever-present problem for me now and will be until the two children I am supporting now are self-determining. I intend to learn and write as much as I can and to survive.

My future plans include a campaign for County Council in 1983-4 Through my work with women and with handicapped people, I can see that priorities must change so they fit human needs. I would rather work for that than anything else I can think of.

Ah, Ginny, I had no idea you had such a background. I hope and expect that we Ginny will be good friends & that you will teach me many things. I worry that this class is not your speed. I have a couple of ideas for us to consider. First, is my giving you your own assignments, &

perhaps having discussions w/ you & perhaps a few others, individually. (We could talk on the phone or in the cafeteria. The other idea is that you collaborate w/ me as co-teacher. I'm sure you and I share a great deal in values & "quest," Ginny. So help me w/ your feedback, insights, ideas, participation, brainstorms, etc., to make HCC So 100 a "consciousness raising" experience for these students.

    I must talk w/ you! And how can I help you?

                Noelie

"The Crooked House An Examination of Sexism in Western Political Thought"

This paper was written by Virginia in April, 1983 for Dr. Richard Keim's Political Science 301 course at the University of Hawaii, Hilo, Hawaii. It is fifteen page research paper on the subjugation of women beginning with Aristotle and Plato. Her introductory paragraphs are especially wonderful:

"In examining my feelings while listening to many lectures in which 'history of man,' 'mankind,' 'man's future,' 'man's political ideas' were spoken of, and after talking to various professors, I became aware that the process was like being shown a house which looks out-ofplumb, or crooked. And, the more I observed that the house looked crooked, the more carefully I was asked to observe it, or parts of it, as though by further examination or study, it would not appear crooked any longer.

The crookedness of the house refers to the pervasiveness of sexism in Western political thought, from Plato and Aristotle to the founders of liberalism, Hobbes, Locke, Rousseau and John Stuart Mill. As we see, sexism extends to other writers largely because of the assumptions made by Plato and Aristotle about the 'nature' of women which in reality examined only the function of childbearing and then took for granted an entire male support system which followed from that function. Like slavery, female labor was (and is) such a fundamental part of the fabric of society, that to allow slaves or females the choice of full participation as citizens would have severely threatened any political system…"

The Crooked House

An Examination of Sexism in

Western Political Thought

By

Virginia Aste

Dr. Willard Keim
Political Science 301
April 1983

The Crooked House
An Examination of Sexism in Western Political Thought

In examining my feelings while listening to many lectures in which "history of man," "mankind," "man's future," "man's political ideas," were spoken of, and after talking to various professors, I became aware that the process was like being shown a house which looks out-of-plumb, or crooked. And, the more I observed that the house looked crooked, the more carefully I was asked to observe it, or parts of it, as though by further examination or study, it would not appear crooked any longer.

The crookedness of the house refers to the pervasiveness of sexism in Western political thought, from Plato and Aristotle to the founders of liberalism, Hobbes, Locke, Rousseau and John Stuart Mill. As we will see, sexism extends to other writers largely because of the assumptions made by Plato and Aristotle about about the "nature" of women which in reality examined only the function of childbearing and then took for granted an entire male support system which followed from that function. Like slavery, female labor was (and is) such a fundamental part of the fabric of society, that to allow slaves or females the choice full participation as citizens would have severely threatened any political system. Slavery has been recognized as an impediment to individual liberty and, as such, was abolished. Recognition of female slavery, or to use a more mild term, unpaid female labor, and inferior status as an impediment to individual freedom has been much slower, and its abolitional, would severely threaten any existing political system.[1]

Feminist writers made me aware of the misogyny in the portrayal and treatment of women throughout history. Footbinding, witch-burning and genital mutilation were used to oppress women. Footbinding had its Western counterpart in iron corsets and chastity belts. Andrea Dworkin calls the 13th Century <u>Malleus Maleficarum</u>, a monument to Aristotle's logic and academic methodology. It describes "the several Methods by which Devils through witches Entice and Allure the Innocent to the Increase of that Horrid Craft and company," Dworkin adds that 9 million people were killed because they were deemed to be witches and the ratio of women to men executed was 20 to 1 or higher.[2] Genital mutilation is still with us in the 1980's, with male judges unable to make decisions to abolish it because it may destroy male-imposed cultural traditions and cause political repercussions.[3] Merlin Stone describes the process by which the female goddesses were deposed and replaced by male godheads.[4] She examines the religious writers (male) who became fanatics in their insistence in portraying women as instigators of evil acts, a concept that is present in Greek and Roman writings and echoed by some historians, namely Toynbee[5] and Mommsen.[6]

Specific examination of the place occupied by women in Western political thought has now been done by Susan Moller-Okin and Marie-Louise Janssen-Juriet, and it is their books which form the basis for this paper. Other American European women wrote about the problem of excluding half the population from political theory and practice much earlier, and both writers mention these authors. Alice Rossi has collected some of those writings in <u>Feminist Papers</u>, where it was perceived that the traditional, male-dominated political house was out-of-plumb. Even now, we cannot assume that gender terms are generic unless we examine what the philosopher says about women.

2

Mary Wollenstonecraft in <u>Vindication of the Rights of Women</u>, published in 1792, observes:

> "To account for, and excuse the tyranny of man, many ingenious arguments have been brought forward to prove, that the two sexes, in the acquirement of virtue, ought to aim at attaining a very different character: or, to speak explicitly, women are not allowed to have sufficient strength of mind to acquire what really deserves the name of virtue. Yet it should seem, allowing them to have souls, that there is but one way appointed by providence to lead <u>mankind</u> to either virtue or happiness."

She points out the inequality of education prescribed for women by Western political thinkers, particularly Rousseau, and emphasizes that it is the quality of education given, rather than the method which leads human beings to their highest achievements. She feels it is no surprise that women fail to reach the achievements when their education is based on "manners before morals," and likens them to trained army personnel, who:

> "Acquire a little superficial knowledge, snatched from the muddy current of conversation, and, from continually mixing with society, they gain, what is termed a knowledge of the world; and this acquaintance with manners and customs has frequently been confounded with a knowledge of the human heart . . . Where is then the sexual difference, when the education has been the same; All the difference that I can discern arises from the superior advantage of liberty which enables the former (the soldier) to see more of life."

She reiterates a common definition of a benevolent legislator:

> "always endeavor(ing) to make it the interest of each individual to be virtuous; and thus private virtue become(es) the cement of public happiness, and an orderly whole is consolidated by the tendency of all the parts towards a common centre. But the private or public virtue of woman is very problematical; for Rousseau, and a numerous list of male writers insist that she should all her life be subjected to a severe restraint, that of propriety."

and then asks, "Why subject her to propriety -- blind propriety, if she be capable of acting from a nobler spring, if she be an heir of immortality? . . . Is not this indirectly to deny woman reason? for a gift is a mockery, if it is unfit for use."

3

Women have become citizens in every country in the world and in most, they have the right to vote. It is undeniable, however, that they have remained second-class citizens if we measure in terms of the characteristics traditionally valued for citizens: education, economic independence, occupational status and political participation.

Two quotes, one from a 20th Century feminist poet, who echoes the thoughts of many women, and the second from a fascist demagogue, reflect the way in which history influences people. If they are unable to see themselves reflected in it, what role models are they to follow? Conversely, if the role models they see reflect men as the center of the universe, what values will they adopt? Janssen-Juriet suggests that they will adopt male values, or more accurately, the female values set for women by men.

> My history books lied to me,
> they said I didn't exist.
>
> -- Alta

> The kind of historical thinking that was
> taught to me in school did not abandon
> me in the period afterward. Increasingly,
> world history became for me an
> inexhaustible source of insights for
> historical action in the present, as well as
> for politics.
>
> -- Adolph Hitler

Women are often excluded from the "required" list in courses because it is difficult to see where they "fit in." Their writing is often a combination of personal observation, history and social commentary, which cuts across disciplines (but so was Plato's). They are also excluded because their works are unknown

4

to male (and female) instructors, whose history books ~~like~~ *lied* to them by telling them that women had non-existent or inferior views.

Two questions come up as we look at the existing tradition of political philosophy: Whether that tradition can sustain the inclusion of women in its subject matter, and, why political enfranchisement of women has not led to substantial equality between the sexes.

It is apparent that most theories can sustain the inclusion of women if we simply examine arguments about freedom and change the gender of the pronoun written, which is almost inevitably male. Closer examination of most theories, however, requires that exercise of the right to education, economic equality, occupational parity and political participation, is expected to take place under the supervision of a male head-of-household. Even if the particular theory does not require this, the fact that so many theories did and that this view is still extremely prevalent in all societies, means that women are effectively denied the basic rights traditionally considered necessary for citizens.

Thomas Hobbes' political philosophy is founded on the argument that human beings beings are naturally equal, on account of the fact that they are equally able to kill one another. He includes women, *in this argument for equality,* repudiating the claim that in nature, dominion belongs to the father. He then justifies the rule of fathers over their families in the commonwealth by pointing out that, "for the most part Commonwealths have been erected by the Fathers, not by the Mothers of families."[6A] He does not answer the question of how half of a race, all of whom are equal by his definition, came to found a commonwealth in which they had dominion over the other half.

5

John Stuart Mill's predecessor, James Mill, argued the rationality of maintaining that the nature of the two sexes adapts them to their present functions and position, and this was a radical departure from the functionalist definitions laid down by previous writers. He has a problem granting universal franchise to women, however, and in "Government," where he examines Bentham's suffrage argument, he observes that "all those individuals whose interests are indisputably included in those of other individuals, may be struck off without inconvenience," and specifically mentions children and women, "the interest of whom is involved either in that of their fathers or in that of their husbands." [6B]

John Stuart Mill violated even the utilitarian definition of the development of human society and compares its development to "a tree, which requires to grow and develop itself on all sides."[6C] He goes on to describe the development of women as a tree which has been grown with one half in a vapor bath and the other in the snow, "forced repression in some directions, unnatural stimulation in others," with the aim of pleasing and benefitting man (non-generic).[6D] His feminism became more prounounced as his life progressed, in contrast to Plato, who became much less sure about the inclusion of women in political life after he wrote the Republic. Harriet Taylor, Mill's wife, perceived the injustice involved in institutions which allowed a man to have a career and economic independence and a home life and children, but which forced a woman to choose between the two.[6E] Mill did not appear too uncomfortable with this lack of choice, presumably because it was not imposed on him.

6

This inconsistency is the same as that which faced John Locke, who presents women as equal for some purposes, but ultimately reverses himself. "Although he uses parental equality to combat absolutism in the political realm, Locke peremptorily concludes in other passages that the is 'a Foundation in Nature' for the legal and customary subjection of women to their husbands," 6E Having jumped squarely into Aristotle's lap, he goes on to affirm that in "things of their common Interest and Property," should a disagreement arise between man and wife, "the Rule . . . naturally falls to the Man's share, as the abler and the stronger."6F

Johann Jakob Bachofen, a mystical historian, turned the whole argument around and maintained that man was created from woman:

> ". . .woman and man do not appear simultaneously, and are not formed together . . . the woman is formed earlier, the man relates to her as a son; the woman is the given, the man is that which first came into being through her . . . the woman is unchangeable; the man is becoming, and therefore always falling to ruin. . . This is the model and foundation of matriarchy." 6G

Bachofen inspired fascist writers, whose idea of matriarchy was in reality a male defined cult of woman which "far from precluding warlike bravery . . . vastly encouraged it."6H He also inspired Engels, who described him as a "mystic of genius", presumably because both believed that women were the instigators of marital intercourse and inheritance rights, a concept which may have originated from Plato. (See Appendix). Bachofen constructed an epoch in which women ruled, but it was not based upon any intellectual equality with men. It was simply a restatement of the functionalist view which Aristotle used to justify women's place in the human hierarchy and a glorifaction of the child-bearing role.

7

Both Marx and Engels (not to mention Rousseau) experienced difficulty in their personal lives with their own procreative capacity versus their ability or desire to care for children, yet neither of them considered adequate contraception a given in their theories. Engels felt that since women could enter the workforce, there would be "no basis for any kind of male supremacy . . . in the proletarian household,"[7] but then he adds, "except, perhaps for something of the brutality towards women that has spread since the introduction of monogamy."[8] He leaves the question of proletarian male brutality unanswered and a number of other social and psychological reasons for female oppression unanswered as well.

In *Capital*, Marx makes it clear that the addition of women to the workforce will cause, "the break-up of the old family system within the organism of capitalist society." He then adds that this change, "is building the new economic foundation for a higher form of the family and of the relations between the sexes."[9] He does not specify what that higher form is except to assume that it will appear when class differences disappear.

Even in countries which have supposedly attained a dictatorship of the proletariat, it does not appear that there is much evidence of this type of transformation. We are unable to get reliable information on spouse and child abuse, although we can see differences in work status between men and women and there is a notable lack of women in positions of political power.

August Bebel and Engels both reasoned that electrical appliances would do away with housework and free women to pursue other interests. Nowhere is it suggested that all aspects of housework would disappear or that any parts of it would be shared by or paid for by other family members. Women of the socialist future would produce like a man and retain typically female functions besides (educator, teacher, nurse), incidentally producing a work of art or . . . scientific literature."[10A] A further blithe statement indicates that:

> "Women is free, and her children, if she has any, do not impair her freedom: they can only fill all the fuller the cup of her enjoyments and her pleasure in life. Nurses, teachers, female friends, the rising female generations -- all are ready to help the mother when she needs help."[11]

Janssen-Juriet points out that the combination of interest in suffrage, pacifism, economic equality and political participation, led many women to write and speak in favor of establishing a separate women's party in the Weimar Republic. Many times, when international women's congresses to discuss these concerns were called, women were denied visas or prevented from attending in other ways, because these goals were threatening to _all_ countries.

As Hitler gained power in Germany, he was able to draw upon the racism and nationalism themes present in Bachofen (Mother's Right) and Wagner to organize opposition to the democratic pluralism which was emerging out of the Weimar Republic. Chauvinism was a powerful addition to the two dominant themes and there was absolutely no doubt that Hitler and other Nazis felt the sole purpose for women was to produce sons for the Third Reich. Emma Goldman, American anarchist spoke out against enfranchisement of women without political power and maintained that only the "refusal to be a servant of the church, of the state, of the society of the husband, of the family, etc., only this, not the ballot, will liberate women."[12] This refusal would have been a death sentence after Hitler came to power, and it was a political death sentence for many women who attempted to combat his rise, and who pointed out the same tendencies in the parties in power prior to Hitler's rise.

9

There has been a great deal written by all of the philosophers considered here on the subject of women and their proper role and station in society. Perhaps more important, is the fact that many philosophers and historians never considered women at all, considered them in a negative way, and most amazing, were never moved to wonder at the omission or the assumption that men were tempted into horrendous deeds or bad decisions by women.

It is important to again emphasize that the ideas of political philosophers are closely connected to their views of the family. Even in the works of those who questioned the value of the family, Robert Owen, Marx, Engels, among others, confusion, ambiguity and assumptions about women caused unequal application of their doctrines to women. Since they were the primary beneficiaries of the support system inherent in the family, it is no wonder that they did not question its value. The freedom which they took for granted enabled them to develop in harmony with the societal norms, whereas women's development was limited, and opposed by those same norms, relegating it (as Simone DeBeauvoir says) to the category of "Other."[12A]

"Charles Fourier first used the status of women in a society as the measure of its advancement and considered the progress of women to be a fundamental cause of general social progress."[13] Okin says. Another feminist historian says, "By the beginning of recent history, authoritarian societies had discovered that by disciplining sexual relationships it was possible to exercise control over the family that contributed usefully to the stability of the state."[14] Few political theorists perceived the degree of oppression present in the patriarchal family system.

Assuming the family to be "natural," and necessary, defining women by their sexual, procreative and childrearing functions within the family, and imposing a corresponding moral code (usually a double standard) led to a particularly limited concept of rights for women which was different from the rights offered to men. Men were seen as having the capacity and the opportunity to use intelligence, reason and expression of those qualities to guide themselves and all other human beings. Women were seen as perhaps having the capacity, but were denied the opportunity to use intelligence and reason except to guide their children, and then only within the sphere approved of by their husbands, brothers or fathers.

The biological differences between men and women dictate all other differences in sex roles which the patriarchal family requires. To this day, many writers cannot separate childbearing from child rearing and insist that there is a biological proclivity toward the latter which women possess. This "biology-as-destiny" role was justified by Freud, whose treatment theories for women still dominate the psychiatric profession. Many women were imprisoned in institutions and shut away from society by men who could not reconcile "their" women's resistance to the patriarchal system, particularly if those men were members of the clergy.[25]

(Philosophers) "have sought for the nature of women not, as for the nature of men, by attempting to separate out nature from the effects of nurture, and to discover what innate potential

11

exists beneath the overlay which results from socialization and other environmental factors. The nature of women, instead has been seen to be dictated by whatever social and economic structure the philosophers favor and to be defined as whatever best suits her prescribed functions in that society . . . asking 'What are men like?' and 'What are women for?'"[16]

"How did theorists resolve these contradictions? Often they did not, and some continue to ignore basic contracidtions into our own time. If equality was important, the inequality of women was concealed by the adoption of a male headed family, rather than taking the individual adult as the first unit to be considered."[17] Plato's confusion and eventual manipulation of the family between the creation of the Republic, the description of its possible decline and the later outline of women's role in the Laws is a case in point. (See Appendix.)

If liberty was important, it was assumed that since women were under the male protection all their lives, their liberty consisted of obedience to males who would exercise their own liberty. Economic independence was sometimes possible, but until fairly recent times, no woman was encouraged by any philosopher to live alone and independently.

Political participation was never seen as a female right, although some women became powerful as "wives of" or as courtesans. Some inherited political power after the death of the husband who had attained it through inheritance or election.

Education produced more ambiguous reactions in political theorists. Rousseau, who wrote a great deal about education, because he believed that historically, education had corrupted men, allowed his heroes to educate themselves and also entrusted them with the task of educating women. He believed in a woman's "right" to an education, but it was not bestowed in the same spirit to women as it was to men. (See Appendix)

In law, discrimination against women was and is upheld by echoing the functionalist treatment of women. Modern judges use arguments parallel to those of Aristotle and Rousseau to limit equal exercise of human capacities for women:

> "The present generation of our younger male population has not become so decadent that boys will experience a thrill in defeating girls in running contests, whether the girls be members of their own team or an adversary team. It could well be that many boys would feel compelled to forego entering track events if they were required to compete with girls on their own team or adversary teams. With boys vying with girls . . . the challenge to win and the glory of achievement, at least for many boys, would lose incentive and become nullified." 18

It must be added that the "challenge to win and the glory of achievement" in male sports is losing its appeal for many males. Whether women will continue to compete in sports and develop a parallel "industry" of team sports remains to be seen.

In assessing why enfranchisement has not led to equality, we could look to the fact that women are in a similar position as citizens in a newly independent nation. They may have unequal access to information enabling them to make choices, they may experience coercion which determines how they will exercise their political choices, or they may simply lack transportation or child care which would enable them to get to the voting place. We could also look to the fact that enfranchisement does not guarantee uniform participation for either sex in the process of government.

13

Often, after political enfranchisement has occurred, it is apparent that it is more of a status symbol than a real political tool. Many newly independent countries are unable to sustain any kind of plurality and become political dictatorships, which do not guarantee human, much less political rights, for anyone. In some countries, female participation is guaranteed, but the female delegates are elected by male legislative bodies (Bangladesh).[1]

A quarter of a million women (and men) now belong to the largest feminist organization in the world (National Organization for Women) and were instrumental in again introducing the Equal Rights Amendment, "Equality of rights under the law shall not be denied or abridged on account of sex." The most surprising thing about the struggle to have it adopted has not been the opposition of men, but the indifference, fear and outright opposition of some women. Clearly, political theories alone do not change people's behavior. Social and psychological pressures are equally strong and the reinforcement for the functionalist view of women's behavior will be present as long as women bear children. Speculation as to the fate of women if medical technology makes test-tube baby production possible on a large scale is something only a few feminist writers have begun to speculate on, but certainly the functionalist argument would be dealt a heavy blow.

We are either part of the problem or part of the solution, as the saying goes. "Where social change is concerned none of us can be neutral: we either contribute to changing the status quo or we help maintain the culture's oppression . . . The change process begins with an awareness of the extent to which cultural expectations set limits for sex-linked behavior."[20] When this realization is an experienced part of many individual personalities, the institutional change will follow and the political philosophies which we are considering here will offer new insights or self-destruct.

<u>Rosenkrantz and Guildenstern are Dead</u>, and <u>Fiddler on the Roof</u>, are two theatrical examples of what happens when the conventional, supposedly logical, certainly functional, fabric of society is disrupted by looking at it from the viewpoint of the minor, rather than major characters, in the first instance, or by challenging traditional patriarchy with historical incidents which demand new solutions, in the second.

Virginia Woolf speaks of economic independence and the difference it makes for women personally and artistically, in <u>A Room of One's Own</u>. She also speculated on the fate of Shakespeare's sister (if he had one) as she takes her plays from theater to theater, without the economic support of father, brother or husband.

It does no good to blame one sex for the fact that political philosophy, along with all other intellectual pursuits, have been considered the exclusive province of men, but with women now entering the field and bringing with them the tools to fix the "crooked house," we can certainly began to place blame if those commentaries and the little known ones which preceded them, are ignored as we continue teaching the history of political thought.

Contributions which women have made and continue to make to world thought must be seen not as a parallel structure, or as "additional insights" into male philosophy, but as views of human history which will balance, enrich and perhaps supplant what we have now.

NOTES

1. John Kenneth Galbraith, "Interview with Gloria Steinem," *Ms. Magazine*, April 1983, p. 27

2. Andrea Dworkin, *Woman Hating*, (New York, 1974), p. 126.

3. *Time Magazine*, _____, 19____, p. ___.

4. Merlin Stone, When God Was a Woman, (_____, 19___,)p. ___.

5. Marie-Louise Janssen Juriet, *Sexism*, (New York, 1982) p. 31.

6. Ibid., p. 32

6A. Susan Moller-Okin, *Women in Western Political Thought*, (Princeton University Press: 1979) p. 198.

6B. Ibid., p. 209

6C. Ibid.,

6D. Ibid.

6E. Ibid., p. 230.

6Ee. Ibid., p. 200.

6F. Ibid.

6G. Janssen-Juriet, p. 53.

6H. Ibid., p. 55.

7. Ibid., p. 109.

8. Ibid.

9. Ibid. p. 110.

10. Ibid., p. 168.

10A. Ibid.

11. Ibid., p. 169.

12. Ibid., p. 150.

12A. Simone DeBeauvoir, *The Second Sex*, (_____, 19__), p. ___.

13. Okin, p. 7.
14. Reay Tannehill, *Sex in History*, (New York, 1980), p. 235.
15. Phyllis Chesler, *Women and Madness*, (New York, 1975), p. 20.

16 Okin, p. 7.

17 Ibid.

18 Alice G. Sargent, Beyond Sex Roles, (West Publishing Co.: 1977), p. 434.

19 Janssen-Juriet, p. 150.

20 Sargent, p. 9; p. 15.

"Sex In History by Reay Tannehill Commentary by Ginny Aste History 398B"

This is a six page paper Virginia wrote on Tannehill's work. She begins with a quote from Tannehill, "'The modern world has had to adapt to almost complete legal and sexual equality in less than a decade. Predicably, the results have been chaotic and the psychological penalty is now having to be paid.'"

Virginia's conclusion is interesting:

"...I feel that Tannehill's conclusion overlooks economic considerations when she says that American women who try to enter public life often must contend with a feminist backlash and then asks if it is a continuation of Neolithic times 'when men did the talking and women got on with the work,' or a genetic demonstration of male superiority.

I find the book more valuable at each reading if only for amusing and little known insights in the complex nature of human sexuality. Tannehill's research is thorough and the questions she raises, even if there are no answers at present, shed light on the feminist course for the next decade or more."

SEX IN HISTORY
by Reay Tannehill
Commentary by Ginny Aste
History 398B

"The modern world has had to adapt to almost complete legal and sexual equality in less than a decade," Reay Tannehill observes. "Predictably, the results have been chaotic and the psychological penalty is now having to be paid."

She traces the twisted and convoluted path of human sexual behavior through prehistoric times and through segments of history and major populations to the present, showing how sexual behavior has evolved and been manipulated for political ends.

Tannehill's work shows how authoritarian societies (and almost all early societies were elitist and authoritarian) discovered that by disciplining sexual relationships it was possible to exercise control over the family which was the fundamental contributor to the state, in a variety of ways.

"Because religious and secular law were so closely intertwined, the morality of sex -- a purposeful myth that has been productive of more guilt and misery than any other aspect of divine law -- has remained an important factor in social control," she states.

Tannehill's survey begins with the prehistoric world, showing the establishment of an incest taboo and menstrual cycle taboos. She traces the development of man-as-hunter and woman-as-gatherer/caretaker. She cites bi-pedal locomotion and frontal sexual posture as two factors establishing male dominance. "My son," and "my wife," she feels, came from man's knowledge of his role in procreation.

Tannehill then traces attitudes, mores and sanctions on sexual conduct through the Near East, Egypt and Europe, showing that the original separation of duties between male and female was maintained and compounded as early states were formed.

Although Plato and Aristotle, the earliest political scientists have opposing views of women's capabilities, they both agreed on the major role for women and it was not to head the state. It was to bear children, and to keep the household in order for the master and for the state. In Plato's <u>Republic</u>, women classed as "gold" and "silver" were to be selected to guardians and auxiliaries of an elite corps who governed the state, owned no property and bore children with pre-selected pairings at times prescribed by the state. Plato said that he believed in woman's capacity to do any work which a man could do, but he also believed women to be physically weaker and never specifies how the transition was to occur from what existed in Athens in his day and his vision in the <u>Republic</u>.

2

Aristotle was largely responsible for the biology-as-destiny view of women which is still held today by many men (and women). He believed women were deficient in their inability to produce sperm, their capacity as vessels or receivers and that women were physically weaker by nature.

The Christian Church grafted itself onto the crumbling Roman Empire and the teachings of Jerome, Tertullian and Augustine (all of whom led full sexual lives before their Christian conversions) made sex a sin except for procreation, and laid (!) the foundation for attitudes about sexuality which still endure today. The ability of the Church to build and sustain these attitudes was due to the vehemence with which these and other church fathers repudiated sexuality and the fact that they controlled the dissemination of written information. Ideas with which they did not agree, simply did not get circulated.

China, India and Islam all agreed on the role of woman, but sex (for men at least) was seen as a _pleasant_ duty at least until the new-Confucians introduced the same system of proscription of pleasure and punishment for sex outside of marriage and for homosexuality.

Tannehill goes on to examine the expanding world and the transference of ideas to the imperial colonies. She remarks that when the Judeo-Christians, via Spain, collided with the pre-Colombian civilizations, the only sin which the Aztecs were not instantly accused of was heresy, and that was because even the Spanish priests couldn't find a way to accuse them of being pagans and heretics at the same time.

She traces the transfer of sexual mores and equipment from one country to another as travel became possible for greater numbers of people. She traces the history of contraceptives from the earliest experiments -- coitus interruptus and coitus obstructus (with crocodile dung!) to the eugenic concepts of early 18th Century advocates like Marie Stopes and Margaret Sanger.

She mentions the brothels operated by the Archbishop of Canterbury and temple prostitution in Avignon and in Rome itself. At the same time, the Church set up "Magdalene homes" for the instruction and rehabilitation of prostitutes. Dual attitudes, it seems, were not uncommon in any historical era, especially in the area of human sexuality.

It is Tannehill's belief that times of great cultural advances do not necessarily mean advances in equality between the sexes. She also points out that times of social upheaval or purposelessness bring about periods of expansion of sexual freedom. Whether sexual freedom can be considered equality is questionable, since in modern times, economic rather than sexual equality seems to be the more desirable goal for women.

Having earler traced the horror with which the Church viewed homosexuality, Tannehill has some interesting remarks about Renaissance attitudes, including a history of the

4

Manichaeans, heretics who forbade sex to the highest ranks, regarded propagation as wrong and left as the sole option homosexual or heterosexual anal intercourse or "buggery." I found this bit of history interesting because Virginia Woolf refers to buggery often in letters quoted in the biography which Clive Bell published a few years ago. Apparently, British socialists were aware of Manichaean theories and some members of Woolf's circle regarded them as a pattern and rationale for turning away from conventional marriage and child raising, thus giving more time to devote to intellectual matters.

Tannehill also talks about contraceptives being accepted, "not as a liberal/humanitarian solution for clearcut social problems, but a factor in class warfare with eugenics as its watchword."

She comments on the "Great Debate" -- suffrage -- and observes that both sides argued that women were "special" and should have (or should not have) the vote for that reason. She further observes that the same reasoning persists in the arguments for and against equality, with Kate Millet and Anita Bryant acting out the respective roles. She points out, as did Susan B. Anthony and Olive Shreiner, that an enemy almost as great as men in judging and deciding what women's limits should be, were (and are) women themselves.

I feel that Tannehill's conclusion overlooks economic considerations when she says that American women who try to enter public life often must contend with a feminist backlash and then asks if it is a continuation of neolithic times "when men did the talking and women got on with the work," or a genetic demonstration of male superiority.

I find the book more valuable at each reading if only for amusing and little known insights in the complex nature of human sexuality. Tannehill's research is thorough and the questions she raises, even if there are no answers at present, shed light on the feminist course for the next decade or more.

> Well done — very nicely written — conveys the scope of the book.
>
> I don't give a grade to these — your grade was given by the class!

"Through The Looking Glass"

This is a ten page research paper Virginia wrote for Dr. Harvey Gochros' Social Work 660 course in the summer of 1990 when she studied for her Master of Social Work degree at the University of Hawaii.

She writes:

"'Through the Looking Glass,' was selected as a metaphor for this paper because Alice's experiences can serve as a reminder that research is filtered through self-knowledge. The constructs 'objective' and 'subjective' are traditional terms which we have been taught to use to describe bias in our research conclusions.

Alice's adventures in the court of the Queen of Hearts describes the dilemma of contemporary women in academic settings. Alice is always the wrong size. If she is little, she needs to be bigger, perhaps to become visible by publishing more. If she is big, she needs to be smaller, less visible, less 'strident,' perhaps less talkative. Alice finds it difficult to get people to hear what she has to say, much less to get her work printed. Her academic life may be threatened precisely because she asks questions which threaten the foundation of what, for her, may become an alien world."

Virginia continues and writes:

"Economics alone have influenced the longevity of women's published work, because it did not 'fit' and because readership was low, making publishing unprofitable. Some of the work of early feminists was lost because, although it might have been published in broadside originality, it was not considered worth republishing in lasting form. Much of women's 'her' stories have been reconstructed from diaries and letters published posthumously by daughters or granddaughters.

A fundamental aspect of feminist research is to examine the function of gatekeeping and to develop strategies to assure that women are equally represented among the 'keepers.' A strategy developed by feminists to address bias and inequality in gatekeeping and publishing has been to publish articles along with the comments included with previous rejections."

Her conclusion is poignant:

"American and European feminists are surprised and dismayed

at the degree of resistance on the part of their male academic colleagues to recognize bias in research concepts, publish more work by women and to integrate feminist writings into their classroom presentations. Third World feminists are dismayed at the degree of resistance by First World feminists to recognize their priorities—food, shelter and freedom from warfare.

Male dominant paradigms, such as patriarchal capitalism, are exhausting world resources, contributing to overpopulation and are creating a planetary future that threatens human existence. New combinations of ecology and feminism and research methods without gender bias may provide answers in terms of cooperation and mutual respect for the plurality and variety of life."

THROUGH THE LOOKING GLASS

BY VIRGINIA ASTE

Dr. Harvey Gochros
Social Work 660
Summer 1990
University of Hawaii M.S.W. Program

"Through the Looking Glass," was selected as a metaphor for this paper because Alice's experiences can serve as a reminder that research is filtered through self-knowledge. The constructs "objective" and "subjective" are traditional terms which we have been taught to use to describe bias in our research conclusions.

Alice's adventures in the court of the Queen of Hearts describes the dilemma of contemporary women in academic settings. Alice is always the wrong size. If she is little, she needs to be bigger, perhaps to become visible by publishing more. If she is big, she needs to be smaller, less visible, less "strident," perhaps less talkative. Alice finds it difficult to get people to hear what she has to say, much less to get her work printed. Her academic life may be threatened precisely because she asks questions which threaten the foundation of what, for her, may become an alien world. It was only a few decades ago that women were excluded from academic pursuits and institutions altogether. One of the beliefs used to substantiate this exclusion was that if women engaged in intellectual pursuits, their reproductive organs would atrophy. (Belenky 1986)

Current research paradigms assume closed systems, shortages of time and resources and they reflect a need to "produce." Because of these presuppositions, traditional research methods not only objectify subjects, but may push the researcher into a position to be objectified by a larger, more powerful entity, a corporation, government or foundation. (Belenky 1986) A feminist view of methodology, on the other hand, upends the concept of "objectivity," maintaining that since the "seers" (theorists and researchers) are members of a particular group (dominant males), the "objective" knowledge gathered in the research must necessarily express the view of that group. Research designed in male dominated institutions like most of our universities and colleges, tends to subsume research about women into the generic, or ignore it altogether. (Belenky 1986)

Whether intentionally or otherwise, research paradigms have resulted in a tradition of dividing human nature into dual and supposedly parallel streams and in the process, attributes traditionally associated with the female gender tend to be ignored. As a result, academics have produced a lot of research about "autonomy and independence, abstract and critical and the unfolding of a morality of rights and justice in both men and women," but there is a lack of research concerning, "the development of interdependence, intimacy, nurturance and contextual thought." (Belenky 1986) The same sociologist comments, "Men gain acceptance into the community of 'thinkers' upon graduation from college, having earned the privilege of having his ideas respected. For women, confirmation and community are prerequisites rather than consequences of development." (Belenky 1986)

Caroline Gilligan, in her book, "In Another Voice," shows that when we listen to women and girls attempt to resolve serious moral dilemmas in their lives, they find solutions inductively, from the particular experiences brought to the situation by each participant, rather than in the traditional male dominant realm of "blind justice" and universal principles. Feminists maintain that objectivity itself is a false concept unless research information is grounded in the factual life experiences of representatives from all human groups and then contrasted to the presuppositions of the researcher, with careful attention to biases as difficult to detect, such as sexism, racism and agism.

INTERVIEWING

The usual instructions for interviews in social science caution the interviewer to keep responses to a minimum, to use responses like "uh-huh," and "tell me more." (Roberts 1981) The interview becomes a "specialized form of conversation in which one person asks the questions and another gives the answers." (Roberts 1981) Women researchers have cited instances where this approach is impossible to sustain because of the crisis nature of the questions from respondents. In interviews of women facing childbirth for the first time, questions were asked which demanded immediate answers and which might have endangered the life of the interviewee had they gone unanswered or been answered by the patronizing textbook standard, "It's my job to get information, not give it." (Roberts 1981)

Feminists point out that instructions given to prospective researchers about "establishing rapport," with the subject is dysfunctional and produces bias because it demands "acceptance by the interviewee of the interviewer's research goals and the interviewee's active search to help the interviewer in providing the relevant information." (Roberts 1981) In other words, the person being interviewed is constantly constructing a third person in the process, one that the interviewer will approve of or who gives the "right" answers.

Adrienne Rich comments, "Where language and naming are power, silence is oppression." Speaking in a prescribed format of hierarchy can be oppressive to women because of the extent to which male authority figures (husbands, clergy, doctors) influence their lives. Isolation and illiteracy are significant variables in the female population. Of the 25 percent of the world's illiterate people, 70 percent are female. Women's language in oral history interviews contain repeated references to "gaining a voice," "saying what you mean," (Belenky 1986), and a woman's response to an interview question might be, "Do you want to know what I think or what society wants me to say?" (Roberts 1981)

All research is subject to bias. Feminists argue that oral histories and interviews conducted on an egalitarian plane instruct in spite of bias. When women complain of loss of selfhood and autonomy under male dominant institutions and research paradigms, men often say they feel the same loss. Alice Yun Chai observes, "A Marxist dialectical approach is reflected in the oral history method. Through life histories, we are able to observe how people adapt to the goals of society ... We learn about behavior that the subject considers meaningful ... Contradictory statements and actions are not necessarily false fronts but manifestations of many levels of social reality." (1985) Both Yun Chai and Ann Oakley comment on the feeling of validation women experience when they have given information about their lives in oral history interviews. Seventy percent of interviewees in Oakley's study said they felt it was reassuring to talk, experienced a change in attitude and said the interviewing process made them think more about the experience of becoming a mother. One of Yun Chai's subjects said, "The only pain worse than recollection was the pain of considering the possibility that the stories would be untold."

Susan Geiger describes the process of recording women's experiences as "writing against the wind," citing Marjorie Shostak's, "Nisa," in which an African tribeswoman gives her the reason for the research endeavor: "I'll break open the story and tell you what is there. Then, like the others that have fallen out onto the sand, I will finish with it, and the wind will take it away." (1986)

ALL THAT FITS, WE PRINT

Bringing women's experiences into the mainstream of sociology, or any discipline, means getting published, but as Dale Spender points out, "While feminists have been acutely conscious of the political dimensions in the construction of knowledge, they have often stopped where the printed word begins." (1981) She further comments, "Academic publishing has often been described in terms of 'gatekeeping,' according to Dorothy Smith, who wrote about publishing in 1978. Gatekeepers are people who set the standards, produce the social knowledge, monitor what is admitted to the systems of distribution and decree innovations in thought, or knowledge, or values."

With publishing comes legitimation, but placing faith in editors to decide what gets printed makes the academic community vulnerable, since there is a publishing hierarchy which impacts upon tenure and promotion. Publication in an academic journal which is supposedly gender neutral, may be perceived to be more valuable in terms of career advancement than publishing in a feminist journal. In reality, the claim of gender neutrality on the part of the academic journal may not survive scrutiny, and the feminist journal may be far more rigorous in its standards. Consequences of career competition for academics via publishing in traditional journals has sometimes resulted in a linguistic style and presentation which moves away from addressing the general, interested reader and which is "oppressive to many ... material that is published does not always reflect genuine concern for the advancement of knowledge." (Spender 1981)

Feminist journals can be exclusionary also and "by staying outside the range of influence of the male gatekeepers, feminists may be faced with two dilemmas." (Spender 1981) First, because they do not have to meet male "standards," feminist material is often seen to be deficient. Second, if they do not submit their material to mainstream journals or publishers, many people have good reason for pleading ignorance when it comes to feminist analysis and insight.

Lillian Robinson, guest lecturer at University of Hawaii Hilo last year, commented on the short-sightedness of author Saul Bellow's when he asserted that he "would read African literature when an African Proust appeared." Robinson was appalled that, "anyone, male or female, would refuse to read or publish a work because it does not conform with a 'Great Books,' concept of a particular discipline." However, she added, "Bellow's views will be followed by some because of his status and another ethnocentric paradigm will be perpetuated." Spender comments, "Gatekeepers are in a position to perpetuate their own schemata by exercising sponsorship and patronage towards those who classify the world in ways similar to their own. Women are by no means the only 'outsiders,' but they are a significant group and there is considerable evidence which suggests that women's schemata does not, at times, 'match' with men's." (1981)

Economics alone have influenced the longevity of women's published work, because it did not "fit," and because readership was low, making publishing unprofitable. Some of the work of early feminists was lost because, although it might have been published in broadside originally, it was not considered worth republishing in lasting form. Much of women's "her" stories have been reconstructed from diaries and letters published posthumously by daughters and granddaughters.

A fundamental aspect of feminist research is to examine the function of gatekeeping and to develop strategies to assure that women are equally represented among the "keepers." A strategy developed by feminists to address bias and inequality in gatekeeping and publishing has been to publish articles along with the comments included with previous rejections.

Silence protects current practices in publishing which discourage feminist dialogue with academia. "Speaking out on a topic that has been shrouded in silence has become a characteristic of feminist research and once more we need to make problematic what has previously been taken too much for granted. We need to do some research on research at the level of publication." (Spender 1981) On the positive side, chapters containing full outlines of feminist theories, written by women are now appearing in sociology textbooks (Ritzer 1988) and an up-to-date summary of feminist thought has been published. (Tong 1989)

INTEGRATION

Identifying feminist perspectives in research methodology and strengthening the ability of feminist writers to publish, leads logically to consideration of another arena in which their work is to be presented -- the classroom. Integrating feminist thought into the curriculum of a college or university was not so difficult when it was considered to be a separate discipline. Courses which focused on marriage and the family, "traditional" areas, were perceived as rightful concerns, but separate. Even when courses on the psychology of women emerged, based on information from and about women, it was not expected that they would affect the entire field of study. Now that a feminist perspective has developed in psychology, history, anthropology, literature and social science, grounded in the life experiences of women, there is a demand for a more comprehensive approach, including a change in research paradigms.

[margin note: or female programs (such as nursing, home ec. etc.)]

The University of Arizona project in interdisciplinary integration of feminist studies was sponsored by the National Endowment of the Humanities and attracted many male faculty members because it paid them under the rubric of "faculty development." Forty-five participants, male, white, middle class, tenured, sat in classrooms with a smaller group of untenured females (feminists) who were mixed in age and ethnicity, but scholastically expert in their fields. The coordinator of the project pointed out that "by situating large numbers of older, generally powerful men as students of younger, less privileged, feminist women, the project reflected in microcosm the power structure of the university itself, while enacting a temporary reversal." (Minnich 1988)

There were successes in the project. Over half of the male faculty accepted the premise that historically women have been treated as second class, and that male bias might be lessened by integrating feminist studies into their courses. In talking about the resistance, Coordinator Susan Aiken observes that some of the professors were curious as to whether scholarship on women was valid. Some engaged in selective reading, hearing and commentary which deflected discussion into tangents and some saw highly diverse discussions by feminist scholars on nature culture and gender as repetitions of the same theme. Resistance was reflected in language, such as the expressions "what to cut," and "shoehorning," (a few courses into an existing structure.) The fact that the group was overwhelmingly male, reinforced the perception of women as figures of "disorder," disrupting the masculine boundary systems. "The academy speaks a language of scholarship, but it also speaks a language of power . . . the discourse becomes inseparable from questions of ownership." (Minnich 1988)
It was not easy to dismiss the women who were conducting the seminars on intellectual grounds and it became necessary to expose the ideology inherent in "neutral" scholarship, which feminist writer Catherine McKinnon has described as "neither neutral, nor neuter."

Jean Baker Miller is quoted by Oakley, putting forth an excellent description of dominant groups:

"A dominant group, inevitably, has the greatest influence in determining a culture's overall outlook -- its philosophy, morality, social theory and even its science. The dominant group thus legitimizes the unequal relationship and incorporates it into society's guiding concepts... Inevitably, the dominant group is the model for 'model human relationships.' It then becomes 'normal' to treat others destructively and to derogate them, to obscure the truth of what you are doing by creating false explanations and to oppose actions toward equality. It follows then, that dominant groups do not like to be told about or even quietly reminded of inequality. Normally they can avoid awareness because their explanation of the relationship becomes so well integrated in other terms; they can even believe that both they and the subordinate group share the same interests and, to some extent, a common experience... Clearly, inequality has created a state of conflict, yet dominant groups will tend to suppress conflict." (Roberts 1981)

One of the conclusions of the Arizona project explains why women find it difficult to be heard in business and in academic settings, even in their own homes, when they attempt to point out inequality or male centered behaviors and philosophies which do not necessarily benefit women. "It is difficult for men to accept that women have been unfairly accorded secondary status in society and simultaneously understand that they have had a part in creating and sustaining such a 'meritocracy.' Refusal or failure to initiate changes creates guilt and dissonance between men's actions and their images of themselves as just and thoughtful people." (Minnich 1988)

Resistance to feminist thought is not confined to Arizona. In a review of a book by Michael Levin, called, "Feminism and Freedom," Stephen Hayward, who calls his review, "The Festering Ideology of Feminism," states that the first stage of feminism in 1848 at Seneca Falls, began "when women began their drive for suffrage and other basic rights... But this form of feminism was reform-minded; its practical political agenda has been wholly achieved, (emphasis added). (Hayward 1988) Hayward then says, "Second stage feminism, aims at nothing less than a revolution in consciousness, and the overthrow of any understanding of nature." What these men say is important for a number of reasons. First, Hayward is the director of journalism at the Claremont Institute for the Study of Statesmanship (sic) and Political Policy. Levin is a professor of philosophy at the City College of New York. Second, they represent and inform gatekeepers and students. Third, at the core of their criticism of feminism is a belief in the "natural" superiority of men, a belief which was introduced by Plato and Aristotle 2,000 years ago and which dies hard. Levin speculates about what would happen if little boys were given dolls to play with and little girls were given footballs. He maintains that feminist thinking is that these little girls, when grown, would be taking steroids and negotiating million dollar contracts. And the boys? Well, he just doesn't see a role for them.

Feminists would be truly surprised to learn that, as Levin believes, "modern feminism has become a working assumption of public policy," especially in view of current statistics about women, children and poverty., a ignorance of the economic and social reality of women's lives is not confined to men since many women shield themselves from the knowledge of worldwide poverty and degradation of women. However, the ignorance is compounded by resistance of the male gatekeepers of the academic community to integrate feminist thought and research into classrooms at all educational levels and by men (and women) who fail to incorporate egalitarian principles into personal lifestyles. It is difficult to invite someone out of the rain if she does not know she is getting wet. Conversely, it is difficult to explain to someone who has an umbrella, that you are getting wet without one (or that he can share it.)

CONCLUSION

In real life, men who adhere to gender stereotypes are likely to find themselves in midlife without a fulfilling plan for their retirement years. Women who make no effort to overcome gender stereotypes are likely to be people who are unable to fill their "empty nests" with constructive, economically productive activity.

In real life, little boys and little girls are being given guns to "play" with in Ireland, Central America and the Middle East. Most of them have never seen a "Cabbage Patch" doll or a football, much less experienced a succession of nutritious meals or lived in a house with running water.

American and European feminists are surprised and dismayed at the degree of resistance on the part of their male academic colleagues to recognize bias in research concepts, publish more work by women and to integrate feminist writings into their classroom presentations. Third World feminists are dismayed at the degree of resistance by First World feminists to recognize their priorities -- food, shelter and freedom from warfare.

Male dominant paradigms, such as patriarchal capitalism, are exhausting world resources, contributing to overpopulation and are creating a planetary future that threatens human existence. New combinations of ecology and feminism and research methods without gender bias may provide answers in terms of cooperation and mutual respect for the plurality and variety of life.

Yes — even though your paper doesn't quite conform to the assignment, you have an important message and you say it well. I especially liked your concluding remarks. We all have a lot to learn.

36/40

Notes & Thanks:

Thanks to Mara Aste and the immediate and extended Brautigan/Aste family; especially to Ianthe Brautigan Swenson's, *You Can't Catch Death, A Daughter's Memoir* (St. Martin's) for the inspiration and view her book generously provides.

Great appreciation is extended to Jennifer Dunbar Dorn for her encouragement, advice, and for the opportunity to help catalog the Edward Dorn archive materials in 2019.

Thanks to Edward Dorn who asked our class if anyone had read Brautigan or had ever heard of him and to raise our hands if so.

Thanks to *Arthur* (online) and *Beat Scene* (print, U.K.) where parts of this manuscript appeared in slightly different form.

Thanks to Susan Ault, Stan Hurst, and Nick Houser, avid young readers of Brautigan on the Walker River Indian Reservation who generously left their books with my parents.

Many thanks to John F. Barber, writer and curator of the *Richard Brautigan Bibliography and Archive* (online) and author of: *Richard Brautigan, Essays on the Writing and Life* (McFarland) for his enthusiasm and scholarship regarding all things Brautigan.

Thanks to the editors at Bottom Dog Press and Beatdom for their suggestions and advice.

Thanks to Andrew Stafford for his online projects.

Much gratitude is given to *Tom Clark Beyond The Pale* and Angelica Heinegg Clark. Duncan Jones, Jonathan Chant, and Nin Andrews are also thanked for early support of *Hawaii Teacher Detective* (my poetry blog).

Thanks to Todd Gunderson for his support!

Thanks to artist Gretchen Grove and her art class at the Wailoa Center in Hilo, Hawaii; for her linoleum block printmaking workshop in 2015 where these prints were created.

Thanks to Raluca Albu, Erica Bodwell, America Hart, Roger Echo-Hawk, Althea Huesties-Wolf, Paul Levitt, Andrei Codrescu, Gabriel Levinson, Tobi Harper, Ray Marsocci, Megan Kruse, Tim Heerdink, and David P. Miller for graciously being willing to read the final phase of this manuscript.

Thanks to Paul E. Nelson and SPLAB for encouragement and support. Thanks to Fred Marchant and his writing courses and also to Colrain writing conferences.

Thanks to Ottmar Hermann Geitner for his support.

Index of photos, artwork, and documents/memorabilia in *Please Plant This Book Coast To Coast*

page ix, photograph of Virginia Brautigan Aste, Ginny Aste Skate Park, Ceremony of Naming and Dedication, Pahoa, Hawaii, 2018. Photo by Susan Kay Anderson.

page x, photograph of Virginia Brautigan Aste, Ginny Aste Skate Park, 2015. Photo by Susan Kay Anderson

page xi, Virginia Brautigan Aste, Black Rock Café, Pahoa, Hawaii, 2015. Photo by Susan Kay Anderson.

page xii, Virginia Bratuigan Aste, Black Rock Café, Pahoa, Hawaii, May, 2009. Photo by Susan Kay Anderson.

page xiii, Virginia Brautigan Aste, Black Rock Café, Pahoa, Hawaii, May, 2009. Photo by Susan Kay Anderson.

page xiv, photograph of Virginia Brautigan Aste, Black Rock Café, Pahoa, Hawaii, 2009. Photo by Susan Kay Anderson.

page 7, photograph of linocut print, "Man's Fate" by Susan Kay Anderson, 2015. Photo by Susan Kay Anderson.

page 8, photograph of linocut print, "Please Plant This Book Coast To Coast #1" by Susan Kay Anderson, 2015. Photo by Susan Kay Anderson

page 10, photograph of linocut print, "Werewolf And Boat" by Susan Kay Anderson, 2015. Photography by Susan Kay Anderson.

page 18, photograph of linocut print, "Please Plant This Book Coast To Coast #4" by Susan Kay Anderson, 2015. Photo by Susan Kay Anderson.

page 29, photograph of linocut print, "Please Plant This Book Coast To Coast #2" by Susan Kay Anderson, 2015. Photo by Susan Kay Anderson.

page 36, photograph of linocut print, Please Plant This Book Coast To Coast #3. 2015. Photo by Susan Kay Anderson.

page 69, photograph of notice in Hawaii Tribune-Herald, Virginia Brautigan Aste run for Hawaii State Representative, 1980s. Courtesy of Virginia Brautigan Aste.

page 70, photograph of poster, Women's Comedy Night, Virginia Brautigan Aste, participant, 1990s. Courtesy of Virginia Brautigan Aste.

page 71, photograph of notice in Hawaii Tribune-Herald, another run by Virginia Brautigan Aste for Hawaii State Representative, 1980s. Courtesy of Virginia Brautigan Aste.

page 72, photograph of Skate Park Crew, 2000s. Gary Safarik (holding sign) backed the skate park in Pahoa during his tenure on the Hawaii County Council. Courtesy of Virginia Brautigan Aste.

page 73, photograph from Blessing Ceremony, Ginny Aste Skate Park. Courtesy of Virginia Brautigan Aste.

page 74, photograph of Dinner In The Park crew, 1990s. Free dinner on Sunday afternoons for six years. Courtesy of Virginia Brautigan Aste.

page 75, photograph of political party run, Green Party, 1980s. Courtesy of Virginia Brautigan Aste.

page 76, photograph of "Domestic Harmony" campaign. This was an attempt to change the language of "domestic violence." 1980s-90s. Courtesy of Virginia Brautigan Aste.

page 77, photograph of State Department of Agriculture Community Garden, Pahoa, Hawaii, 1980s. Courtesy of Virginia Brautigan Aste.

page 78, photograph of Hawaii Kilohana Award for Outstanding Volunteerism, 2002. Courtesy of Virginia Brautigan Aste.

page 79, photograph of first skate park t-shirt, fundraising for the Pahoa Skate Park that was to become the Ginny Aste Skate Park in 2018. Colin Green, far left, Paradise Newland (in hat), Michael Hyson in Aloha shirt. Courtesy of Virginia Brautigan Aste.

page 145, photograph of Virginia Brautigan Aste at Sea Lion Caves, Florence, Oregon, September, 2019. Photo by Susan Kay Anderson.

Virginia Brautigan Aste has a skate park graced with her name in Pahoa, Hawaii. She is a 2015 Friend Of Youth Award Recipient presented by the Hawaii State Teacher's Association's Committee on Civil and Human Rights, a grandmother, community activist, and substitute teacher on the Big Island of Hawaii. This is where she has lived for the past forty years, having raised four children as a single mother. Her eldest, Ianthe, is the daughter of writer Richard Brautigan, to whom she was married. Part of the bohemian scene of 1960's San Francisco, and knowing many of its notorious figures, she was key to launching her husband's early writing, serving as muse, and getting jobs to support them. She has been integral to the development of the Ginny Aste Skate Park, the Women's Center at the University of Hawaii-Hilo, Hilo YWCA, Friends of the Park, and has run for the Hawaii State Senate four times as a representative. She organized and advocated for numerous community projects such as; rights for papaya growers, public library access for Pahoa area students, and lobbied for public facilities improvements for East Hawaii. She was born in Rexburg, Idaho and raised in Reseda, California by her entrepreneurial father, teacher-trained mother and her father's relatives before leaving home at age 16 to see the world at the University of California-Los Angeles, where she had a job on the student publication, *The Daily Bruin*. She remains loyally rooted in her Pahoa community despite evacuating several times due to living in the path of hurricanes and lava on the slopes of a live volcano.

Susan Kay Anderson has won awards, fellowships, and has been short-listed for national writing prizes. She has poems published in *Barrow Street 4 X 2 Project, Caliban Online, Cathexis Northwest Review, Gnashing Teeth, Mojave River Review, Mudfish, Puerto del Sol, Rolling Stock, Sleet Magazine, Square One, Tom Clark Beyond The Pale,* and other publications. Her honors include fellowships from the University of Colorado, Ragdale, Anderson Ranch Center for the Arts, Student Conservation Association, an American Intercultural Field Service Exchange to Finland, and year abroad at the University of Tuebingen. She grew up in Nome, Missoula, Reno, and Germany, among other places, before studying at the University of Oregon and then at the University of Colorado, where her master's thesis, directed by Edward Dorn, earned the Jovanovich Award. She worked as a secondary and post-secondary educator in Hawaii for twenty years and is married to Ottmar Geitner, a painter from Germany. Anderson earned an MFA in Creative Writing at Eastern Oregon University in 2017. Her thesis was directed by James Crews and became her first book of poems, *Mezzanine* (Finishing Line Press, 2019). Anderson has worked as an archeological technician, custodian, educator, barista, deli-worker, farm hand, receptionist, painter, book clerk at Explore Booksellers in Aspen, and at other endeavors. She lives in Sutherlin, Oregon and Eugene, Oregon.

Sea Lion Caves, Florence, Oregon, September, 2019

www.ingramcontent.com/pod-product-compliance
Lightning Source LLC
Chambersburg PA
CBHW040253170426
43191CB00019B/2396